ATLAS OF EARTH

ATLAS OF EARTH

Alexa Stace

Consulting Editor
Dougal Dixon

Gareth Stevens Publishing
MILWAUKEE

Consulting editor
Dougal Dixon

Editor
Alexa Stace

Design
Nigel Bradley

Picture research
Elisabeth Sackett and Nigel Bradley

Illustration
Julian Baker and Lee Rowe

Gareth Stevens series editor
Dorothy L. Gibbs

Produced by AND Cartographic Publishers Ltd
Alberto House, Hogwood Lane
Finchampstead, Berkshire RG40 4RF, United Kingdom

© 1999 AND Cartographic Publishers Ltd.
Additional end matter © 2000 by Gareth Stevens, Inc.

Color origination by Job Color srl, Italy

AND Cartographic Publishers thanks Robert Stacey and Emery
Miller of WorldSat International Inc., Mary-Louise Shmid and
Debbie Dodds of NASA (Johnson Space Flight Center), and Rob
Bauer of the University of Colorado at Boulder (Snow and Ice Data
Center – Cooperative Institute for Research in Environmental
Sciences) for their help in producing this book.

Gareth Stevens Publishing thanks Randall Rohe, Ph.D. for his
assistance with the accuracy of the text. Dr. Rohe is Professor of
Geography at the University of Wisconsin – Waukesha, where he
teaches Physical Geography and Geology. He also has authored
over forty publications in scholarly journals, along with numerous
book reviews, monographs, book chapters, and paper presentations.

This edition published in the United States of America by
Gareth Stevens Publishing
1555 North RiverCenter Drive, Suite 201
Milwaukee, Wisconsin 53212 USA

**For a free color catalog describing Gareth Stevens' list
of high-quality books and multimedia programs, call
1-800-542-2595 (USA) or 1-800-461-9120 (Canada).
Gareth Stevens Publishing's Fax: (414) 225-0377**

Library of Congress Cataloging-in-Publication Data available upon
request from publisher. Fax: (414) 225-0377 for the attention of the
Publishing Records Department.

ISBN 0-8368-2505-5

Printed in the United States of America

1 2 3 4 5 6 7 8 9 04 03 02 01 00

Picture credits

l=left, *r*=right, *t*=top, *c*=center, *b*=bottom

2-3 NASA/Science Photo Library; 5 Julian Baker; 6 NASA/Science Photo Library;
7 NASA; 8 *tl, bl, br* AND, *rc* NASA, *r* Landsat; 9 Planet Earth Pictures; 10 *tc* NASA,
bl NASA/Science Photo Library; 11 *l* NASA, *rb* GSFC/NASA; 12 *tl* AND,
bl NASA/Science Photo Library, *c* AND; 13 *t* AND, *b* AND; 14 *lc* NASA/Science
Photo Library, *bl* AND, *bc* NASA; 15 *l* F. Zullo/Science Photo Library, *r* Julian
Baker; 16 *t* Julian Baker, *b* BP/NRSC/Science Photo Library; 17 *l* Planet Earth
Pictures, *t, c, b* Julian Baker, *r* WorldSat; 18 AND; 19 *bl* AND, *br* ZEFA;
20 *l* NASA, *ct* NASA, *cb* NASA, *r* WorldSat; 21 *c* WorldSat, *tr* Planet Earth
Pictures, *b* Mark Lawson; 22 WorldSat; 23 *lc* NASA, *t* Julian Baker, *rc* NASA,
b Southampton Oceanography Centre; 24 *lc* Planet Earth Pictures/Pascal Tournaire,
lb WorldSat, *tl* NASA, *tr* Landsat, *cl* NASA, *cr* NASA; 25 *tl* Julian Baker, *tr* NASA,
cr NASA, *b* WorldSat; 26 *tl* David Parker/Science Photo Library, *tr* Martin Bond/
Science Photo Library, *lc* Massonet et al/CNES/Science Photo Library; 27 *t* Julian
Baker, *c* NASA, *bl* Popperphoto, *br* Peter Menzel/Science Photo Library; 28 *t* NASA,
b Planet Earth Pictures/John Lythgoe; 29 *l* Adam Hart-Davis/Science Photo Library,
rt Planet Earth Pictures, *rc1* Planet Earth Pictures, *rc2* Natural History Museum,
rb NASA; 30 *t* GSFC/NOAA, *b* AND; 31 *t* Julian Baker, *c* NASA, *br* François
Gohier/Science Photo Library; 32 *tl* NASA, *b* Julian Baker, *tc* Natural History
Museum; 33 *r* NASA, *c* AND, *b* Julian Baker; 34 *t* NASA, *b* Landsat; 35 *l* Julian
Baker, *rt* AND, *rc* AND, *b* Planet Earth Pictures/Ken Vaughan; 36 Landsat/Science
Picture Library; 37 NASA; 38 NASA; 39 *c* NASA, *tr* Julian Baker, *br* NASA;
40 *c* WorldSat, *bl* Science Picture Library, *br* AND; 41 *tl* NASA, *bl* AND, *r* NASA;
42 *l* NASA, *r* Julian Baker; 43 *t* NASA, *b* NASA; 44 NASA; 45 *tl* Julian Baker,
tr Science Photo Library, *b* Julian Baker; 46 *t* NASA, *b* Planet Earth Pictures/Jean
Paul Navicet; 47 *r* Landsat, *b* AND; 48 *l* WorldSat, *tr* NRSC/Science Picture Library,
br Planet Earth Pictures/Jonathon Scott; 49 *lt* NASA, *lc* Landsat, *ct* Landsat,
cr1 NASA, *cr2* NASA, *bl* Julian Baker, *bc* NASA, *r(all)* Snow and Ice Center/
University of Colorado at Boulder; 50 *lc* Spot Image, *bl* AND, *bc* NASA;
51 *tl* Julian Baker, *tr* A. C. Twomey/Science Photo Library, *bc* NASA; 52 *tl* WorldSat,
b AND, *c* Landsat; 53 *tl* AND, *rc* Julian Baker, *b* Landsat; 54 *t* WorldSat, *b* AND;
55 *t* AND, *b* Julian Baker; 56 *l* NASA, *c* NASA, *r* NASA; 57 *lc* AND, *bl* South
American Pictures, *br* NASA; 58 *t* GSFC/NASA, *c* GSFC/NASA, *bl* Planet Earth
Pictures; 59 *t* AND, *b* GSFC/NASA; 60 NASA; 61 *t* Julian Baker, *r* AND, *bl* Planet
Earth Pictures, *br* Planet Earth Pictures/Alex Williams; 62 WorldSat; 63 *lt* Julian
Baker, *lb* Landsat, *r* NASA, *b* NASA; 64 NASA; 65 *t* Julian Baker, *c* NASA,
b Planet Earth Pictures/Gary Bell; 66 NASA; 67 NASA; 68 *l* AND, *b* NASA;
69 *lt* NOAA/NASA, *rt* Julian Baker, *rb* NASA; 70 *t* NASA, *c* NASA, *b* NASA;
71 *c* NASA, *tr* Julian Baker, *br* Planet Earth Pictures/David Ponton; 72 *t* GSFC/
Science Photo Library, *b* NOAA/NASA, *bl* Robert Harding Picture Library;
73 *lt* Julian Baker, *rt* GSFC/NASA, *rc* Science Photo Library, *b* AND; 74 *t* NASA/
Science Photo Library, *b* NASA; 75 *t* Landsat, *b* NASA; 76 *l* NOAA/Science Photo
Library, *c* Science Photo Library; 77 *t* NOAA/NASA, *c* NASA/Science Photo Library,
b NOAA/NASA; 78 NASA; 79 *tr* S. Fraser/Science Photo Library, *c* NASA,
bl V. Vick/Science Photo Library; 80 NASA/Science Photo Library; 82 *t* NASA,
rc NASA, *b* Science Photo Library; 83 *tl* WorldSat, *rc* AND, *b* NASA; 84 *l* WorldSat,
c WorldSat; 85 *t* AND, *b* ESI/Science Photo Library; 86 *t* AND, *c* NASA;
87 *c* WorldSat, *rt* NASA, *rb* NASA; 88 *t* NASA, *b* WorldSat; 89 *t* WorldSat, *b* Spot
Image; 96 WorldSat.

Contents

Introduction

S INCE THE dawn of civilization, people have been trying to understand the world. The earliest maps, produced by the Ancient Greeks, showed the islands and coastlines of the Mediterranean Sea, which was the limit of known travel for their galleys and sailing ships.

The study of mathematics, geology, astronomy, and other sciences brought about more accurate surveying, and, as the world became better known in the Middle Ages, maps of Earth gradually became more detailed and more meaningful.

In modern times, the development of air travel has enabled us to see our living landscape from above. The shapes of islands, courses of rivers, and layouts of cities can now be seen directly.

OUR EARTH –
THE
LIVING PLANET

It has even been possible for astronauts, flying high enough, to detect the actual curvature of the horizon.

We now live in the Space Age. In the late 1960s, the first manned expeditions to the Moon brought back photographs of Earth as a sparkling jewel in the empty, star-studded darkness of infinite space – the entire planet on a single photograph frame.

We send satellites into orbit to look at our world with an array of cameras, scanners, and sensors. Computers analyze their data and present it in photographic form, altered with false colors, to reveal surface features that are invisible in normal light. Besides showing what our world looks like, these photographs have had far-reaching effects in all areas of

WATER AND AIR – ELEMENTS THAT MAKE EARTH UNIQUE

(continued on page 9)

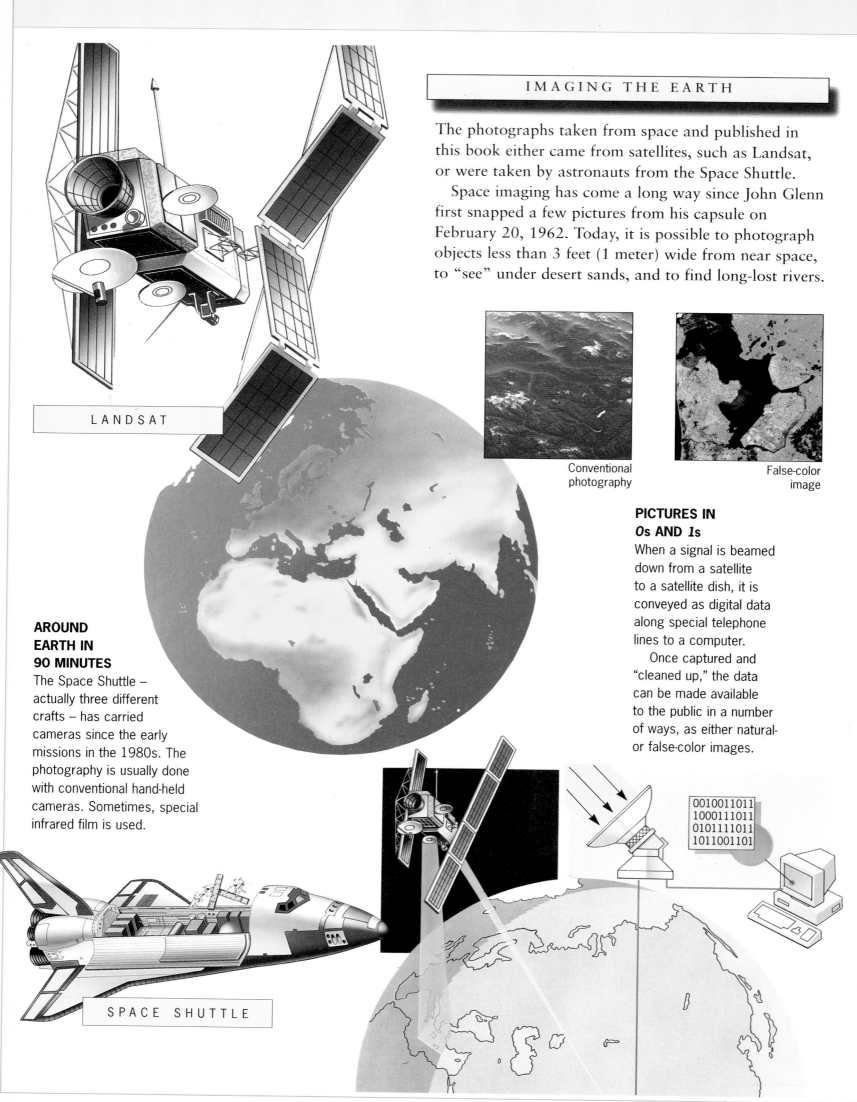

IMAGING THE EARTH

The photographs taken from space and published in this book either came from satellites, such as Landsat, or were taken by astronauts from the Space Shuttle.

Space imaging has come a long way since John Glenn first snapped a few pictures from his capsule on February 20, 1962. Today, it is possible to photograph objects less than 3 feet (1 meter) wide from near space, to "see" under desert sands, and to find long-lost rivers.

Conventional photography

False-color image

LANDSAT

PICTURES IN 0s AND 1s

When a signal is beamed down from a satellite to a satellite dish, it is conveyed as digital data along special telephone lines to a computer.

Once captured and "cleaned up," the data can be made available to the public in a number of ways, as either natural- or false-color images.

AROUND EARTH IN 90 MINUTES

The Space Shuttle – actually three different crafts – has carried cameras since the early missions in the 1980s. The photography is usually done with conventional hand-held cameras. Sometimes, special infrared film is used.

0010011011
1000111011
0101111011
1011001101

SPACE SHUTTLE

environmental study, including agriculture, forestry, mineral and water resources, and urban planning.

Textbook diagrams are valuable in presenting the theory behind geographic features. Now we can back up those diagrams with images from space – to see a river follow its course from the mountains to the sea; to see the march of sand dunes across a desert; to see the different kinds of coral produced as an island chain ages. The elegance, simplicity, and complexity of Earth's natural processes, and the human modification of them, can now be seen directly. We can present a snapshot album of our world!

Dougal Dixon, Consulting Editor

FIRE AND HEAT – NATURE AT ITS MOST SPECTACULAR

PART ONE

The Living Planet

*Earth in the making –
movements in Earth's crust,
its atmosphere, and even outer space
shape our planet.*

Earth in Space

See also:
- **The Air Around Us** *p. 14*
- **Moving Plates** *p. 18*
- **Spreading Rifts** *p. 22*
- **Building Mountains** *p. 24*

WHERE WE ARE IN SPACE

The nine planets of the Solar System are either small and rocky or huge and made of gas. Earth is the largest of the five known rocky planets, four of which lie close to the Sun. Earth is only one-eighth the diameter of Jupiter, the largest of the gas giants.

9 Pluto

8 Neptune

7 Uranus

6 Saturn

5 Jupiter

4 Mars

3 Earth

2 Venus

1 Mercury

THE SUN is Earth's life-giving force, and the distance that separates them is essential for life to exist. The "ecosphere" is the region around the Sun with a suitable temperature to sustain life. Inside the inner boundary would be too hot; outside the outer boundary would be too cold. Earth is at the midpoint, with Venus at the inner edge and Mars at the outer edge. Nowhere else in the solar system is able to support life as we know it. Although the Moon is a similar distance from the Sun, it lacks an atmosphere, so the average temperature is 3°Fahrenheit (-16°Celsius), compared with Earth's 59°F (15°C).

ORBITS IN SPACE

The numbers on these diagrams correspond to the positions of the planets in orbit around the Sun.

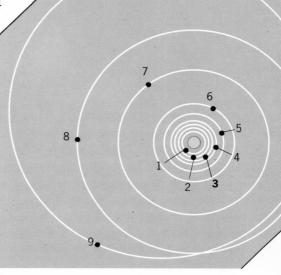

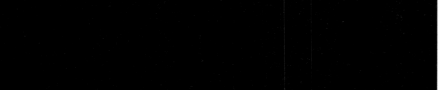

EARTHRISE,
DECEMBER 22, 1968

Left:

As Apollo VIII *orbited the Moon on its pre-landing mission, the astronauts took this picture showing Earth rising above the Moon's horizon. The moonscape is lit orange by the rays of the Sun, which is behind the passing space capsule.*

ONE THEORY

How Earth began has many theories. One theory claims that a star was hit by a passing asteroid.

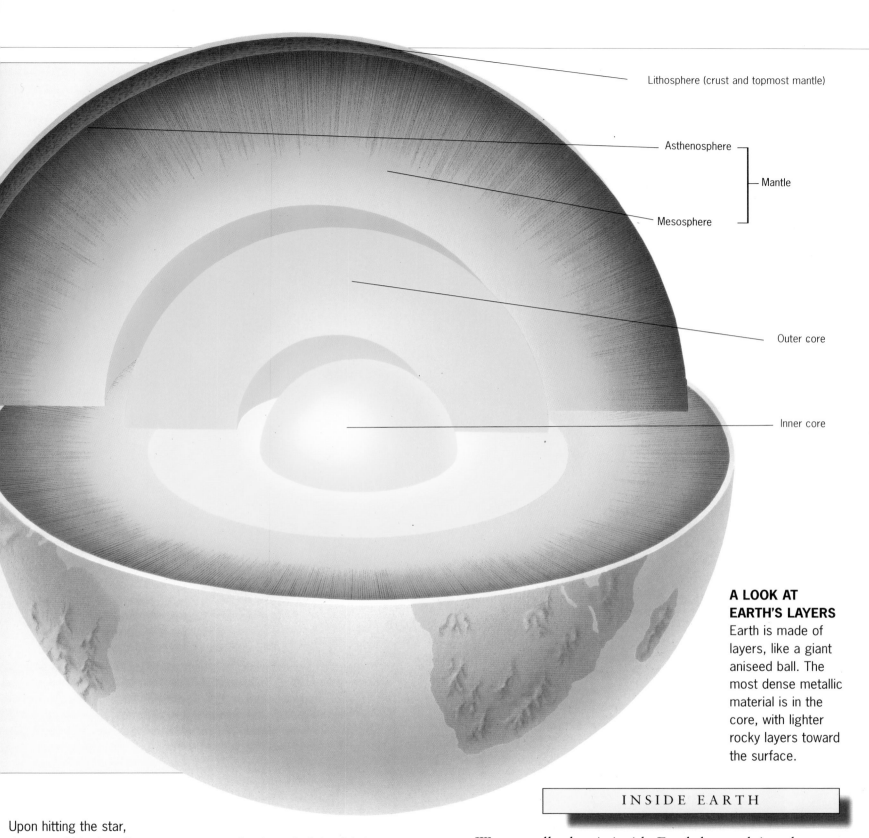

Lithosphere (crust and topmost mantle)

Asthenosphere

Mantle

Mesosphere

Outer core

Inner core

A LOOK AT EARTH'S LAYERS
Earth is made of layers, like a giant aniseed ball. The most dense metallic material is in the core, with lighter rocky layers toward the surface.

INSIDE EARTH

Upon hitting the star, the asteroid broke off a chunk of stellar debris, which was flung away from the star.

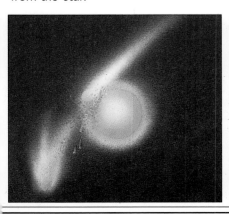

Gravity pulled the debris into the star's orbit, where it cooled down and later became a proto-Earth.

We can tell what is inside Earth by studying the vibrations of earthquake waves. There are two kinds of vibrations – one makes a back-and-forth movement, and the other makes a side-to-side movement. The first kind can pass through layers of solid and liquid, but the second can pass only through solids.

From the studies of vibrations, we know that the center of Earth, the inner core, is solid and is surrounded by a liquid outer core. The main bulk of Earth is a solid rocky mantle, which has a plasticlike area, called the asthenosphere, near the top. Earth's crust, which is the only part we experience directly, is a kind of very thin "rind" around the outside.

The Air Around Us

See also:
- **Fallen Stars** p. 30
- **Rivers** p. 38
- **. . . and Deltas** p. 42
- **Holes in the Sky** p. 76

Sun rays strike the atmosphere and split into various parts.

Below:
This famous image, taken during one of the Apollo missions in the late 1960s, shows the effect of light refracting – splitting into its component parts – in the atmosphere.

THE ATMOSPHERE is the outermost "shell" of Earth's structure. It is composed of a mixture of gases that envelops the whole globe. At first, the atmosphere contained a poisonous mixture of gases such as hydrogen, carbon dioxide, and methane. As plants evolved, however, they absorbed much of the carbon dioxide and produced oxygen, so the atmosphere gradually became as it is today – a mixture of gases able to support animal life.

EARTH'S BLANKET

Without the atmosphere, Earth would be unbearable. The side facing the Sun would roast in the heat; the other side would be freezing. The atmosphere acts like insulation. During the day, it allows sunlight through but filters out most of the harmful rays from the Sun. At night, it traps warmth at Earth's surface and prevents it from radiating into space. Its gases absorb some of the radiation and send energy back to Earth – a balancing process called the "greenhouse effect."

PARTS OF A RAY
1. Most infrared rays pass through Earth's atmosphere.
2. Most ultraviolet rays are reflected away.
3. Light reaches Earth's surface, but some of it is reflected back.
4. The infrared rays that reach Earth's surface are bounced back into the atmosphere.
5. Some of the reflected infrared radiation remains trapped in the atmosphere.

LIFE CYCLES

Earth is a dynamic system with something always happening. Nearly all the chemicals that make up Earth, and the living things on it, have been here since it was first formed, some 15 billion years ago.

Rocks form from fragments of rocks that existed before. Eventually the new rocks decay or are broken down, and their remains form another generation of rocks. It is the same for the living systems. All the substances in an animal's or a plant's life cycle are reused over and over again.

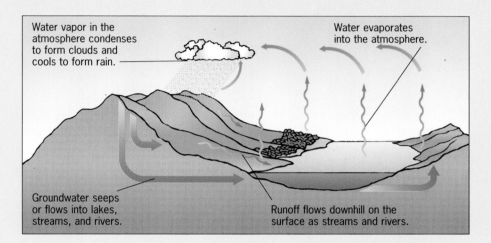

Water vapor in the atmosphere condenses to form clouds and cools to form rain.

Water evaporates into the atmosphere.

Groundwater seeps or flows into lakes, streams, and rivers.

Runoff flows downhill on the surface as streams and rivers.

THE WATER CYCLE

What makes Earth unique is that water is freely available at the surface. It exists in three forms: liquid, solid, and vapor.

Water in the oceans is evaporated by the Sun into vapor. The vapor condenses into clouds of droplets that fall as rain.

Water flows downhill, on the surface (runoff) as streams or through the rocks (groundwater) to emerge as springs, and eventually returns to the oceans as rivers.

Along its route, water is used by animals, plants, and man. It is absorbed into their bodies and returned to Earth when its work is done.

Oxygen in the atmosphere falls to Earth in rain and is breathed in by animals on land.

Photosynthesis, by plants on land and by marine animals in the sea, returns oxygen to the atmosphere.

CARBON AND OXYGEN CYCLES

Life is based on the workings of organic chemistry, which involves the buildup and breakdown of complex carbon-based molecules. Carbon and oxygen are constantly moving around in this system. Carbon is the foundation of all plant and animal life. Oxygen enables living organisms to breathe.

Carbon dioxide is given off into the atmosphere and breathed in by plants to aid photosynthesis.

Decaying plants and animal waste feed the soil.

Above:
A meteorite burns up as it hits Earth's atmosphere. Only on rare occasions do meteorites penetrate this shield.

Left:
The atmosphere is colored by pollutants, suspended dust, and other matter. Here, the sky appears golden red from dust generated by the 1991 eruption of Mount Pinatubo in the Philippines. The dust cloud from this volcano affected a large portion of Earth's atmosphere.

Earth Movements

See also:
- **Moving Plates** *p. 18*
- **Volcano!** *p. 20*
- **Spreading Rifts** *p. 22*
- **Building Mountains** *p. 24*

LIQUID ROCK

Underneath Earth's thin shell lies an enormous, pulsating mass of hot and cool liquid rock on which our continents float. In this computer model, red is hot rock and blue is cool rock. The flows are shown separately for clarity.

Hot magma rises and sometimes escapes through cracks and volcanoes in Earth's surface.

Cooling magma flows down to the center of Earth to be reheated.

HUGE SECTIONS, or "plates," of Earth's hard outer layers produce massive forces as they float on partly molten rock. The slow movement of these plates – no more than about 5 inches (12.5 centimeters) a year – affects the shape of the continents. The forces produced as the plates collide or move apart are responsible, over many millions of years, for the formation of mountains, volcanoes, underwater canyons, and earthquakes.

Volcanoes are formed very dramatically. Molten rock, called "magma," is forced through cracks in Earth's crust. The magma cools quickly into the solid rock of volcanic mountains. Cracks oozing molten lava on the ocean floor build new seabed, while plates rubbing together cause earthquakes.

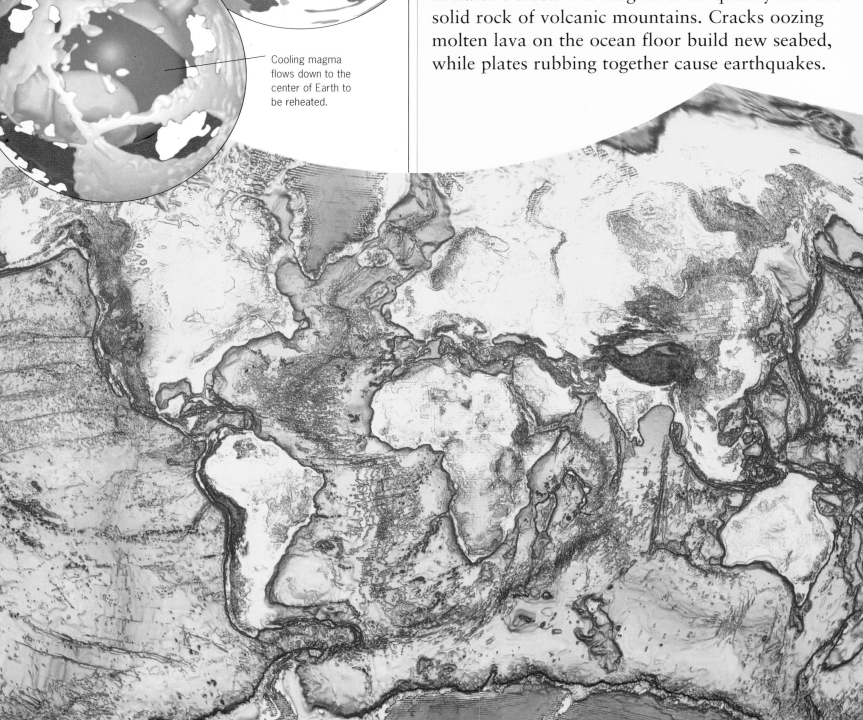

PANGAEA 250M YEARS AGO

HOW EARTH HAS CHANGED

Earth today is very different from what it was 250 million years ago. Then, it was one large landmass, known as Pangaea, with a single ocean, called the Tethys Ocean. Over millions of years, Pangaea split apart, in a process known as "continental drift," into the landmasses, or continents, we recognize today.

JURASSIC EARTH 200M YEARS AGO

CRETACEOUS EARTH 150M YEARS AGO

Left:
Active volcanoes are among the most spectacular sights on Earth. This photograph, taken in Hawaii, shows molten rock from inside Earth's crust oozing out of cracks and slowly cooling.

EARTH TODAY

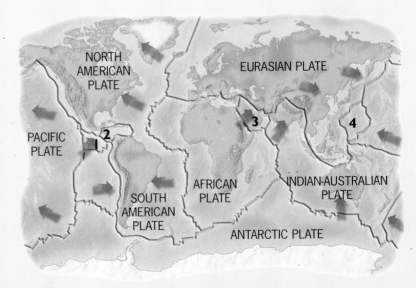

OUR MOVING WORLD

Earth's outer layer, or lithosphere, is made up of seven major plates and a few smaller ones. Many plates consist of both ocean floor and dry land.

This diagram shows the main plate boundaries, the edges where Earth's crust is weakest. Most volcanoes and earthquakes occur at these edges.

Key:

Main plate boundaries		Direction of movement	

 Cocos plate   Caribbean plate  Arabian plate ❹ Philippine plate

NORTH AMERICAN PLATE

EURASIAN PLATE

PACIFIC PLATE

AFRICAN PLATE

INDIAN-AUSTRALIAN PLATE

SOUTH AMERICAN PLATE

ANTARCTIC PLATE

Moving Plates

See also:
- **Earth Movements** *p. 16*
- **Volcano!** *p. 20*
- **Spreading Rifts** *p. 22*
- **Building Mountains** *p. 24*

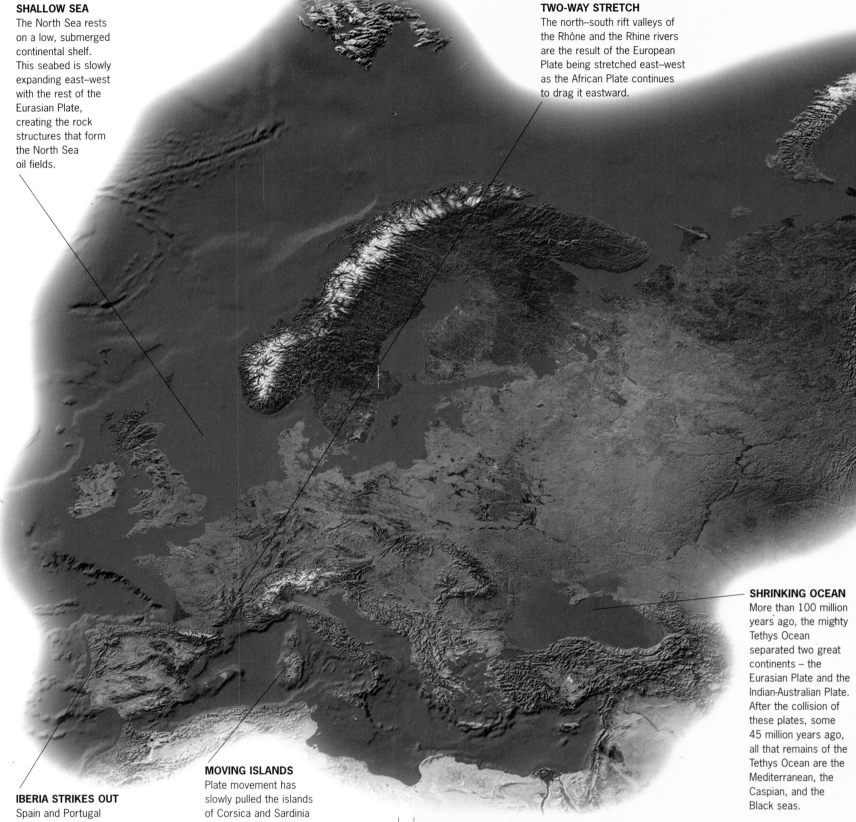

SHALLOW SEA
The North Sea rests on a low, submerged continental shelf. This seabed is slowly expanding east–west with the rest of the Eurasian Plate, creating the rock structures that form the North Sea oil fields.

TWO-WAY STRETCH
The north–south rift valleys of the Rhône and the Rhine rivers are the result of the European Plate being stretched east–west as the African Plate continues to drag it eastward.

SHRINKING OCEAN
More than 100 million years ago, the mighty Tethys Ocean separated two great continents – the Eurasian Plate and the Indian-Australian Plate. After the collision of these plates, some 45 million years ago, all that remains of the Tethys Ocean are the Mediterranean, the Caspian, and the Black seas.

IBERIA STRIKES OUT
Spain and Portugal split away from France, moved south, and swung west. This movement created the Bay of Biscay and crunched the remaining land between Spain and France, forming the Pyrenees Mountains.

MOVING ISLANDS
Plate movement has slowly pulled the islands of Corsica and Sardinia away from the underside of France and Italy and into their present positions.

Above:
Europe, with its valleys, mountains, bays, and islands, is a perfect example of a continent created by tectonics.

THE BARE bones of all the continents are the result of plate movements, past and present. Colliding plates twist up mountain chains, diverging plates wrench continents apart, and active plate boundaries are the sites of volcanoes and earthquakes. The shapes of the continents may seem random, but they all represent the legacy of the worldwide movement of Earth's surface.

SWINGING LANDS

Europe has a solid heart of ancient rock, surrounded by crumpled mountain ranges of younger rock. The younger rocks have been shaped by continuous plate movement. In the last few ten millions of years, the African Plate has moved north, colliding with Europe, squeezing out the ocean between, and throwing up mountain ranges along its northern edge. Now, Africa is moving east, stretching the fabric of Europe east–west.

These rocks were built up about 400 million years ago.

The Baltic shield of ancient rock is partly buried under new rock that forms Belarus, Poland, and much of Eastern Europe.

These rocks were built up about 300 million years ago.

The Atlas Mountains in Morocco, as well as the Apennines in Italy and the Alps and the Carpathian Mountains in Eastern Europe, have been twisted into a continuous S shape as the continents of Europe and Africa have ground past each other.

These rocks were built up about 50 million years ago and are the youngest in Europe. They are also the most earthquake prone and volcanically active.

Today Australia has turned in the opposite direction.

WALTZING MATILDA, WALTZING MATILDA

Australia was originally part of Gondwana, the southern super-continent that also included Antarctica, India, Africa, and South America. Gondwana began to break up about 65 million years ago, splitting into the various continents as we know them now. Australia was the last to move, breaking off from Antarctica about 50 million years ago and drifting northward. It is still moving. Some day it will collide with the mainland of Asia, and vast mountain ranges like the Himalayas will be formed in between.

DRIFTING NORTH
Australia's progress north, as part of Gondwana and as a single continent, can be plotted by examining the magnetism in rocks that formed at certain times.

50 million years ago, after separating from Antarctica, Australia was upside down.

Right:
Marsupials, like this opossum, probably spread from the Americas to Australia via Antarctica, at the time these three continents were joined together.

Volcano!

See also:
- **Earth Movements** p. 16
- **Moving Plates** p. 18
- **Spreading Rifts** p. 22
- **Shake, Rattle, and Roll** p. 26

THE GREATEST forces on Earth can be unleashed when a volcano erupts – or it could be a small stream of molten magma slowly cooling into rock. Such is the unpredictable nature of volcanic activity, which is why volcanoes are so dangerous.

The most famous eruption occurred in Italy in 79AD when Mount Vesuvius smothered the Roman towns of Pompeii and Herculaneum with hot ash. In 1883, Krakatao, an island volcano east of Java, blew apart and disappeared overnight, and in 1991, Mount Pinatubo in the Philippines produced the greatest volcanic explosion of this century.

THE TWO BASIC TYPES OF VOLCANOES

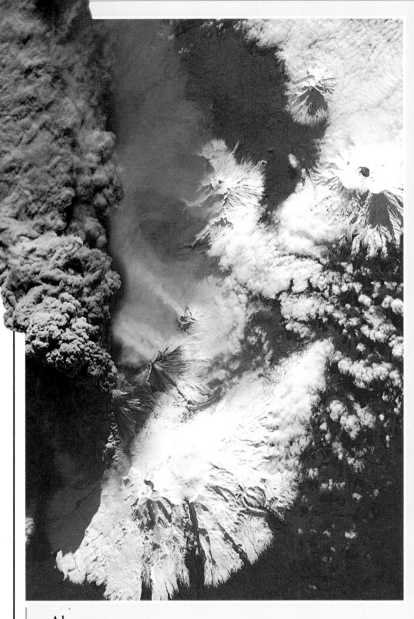

Above:

As the Space Shuttle Endeavour *passed over the Kamchatka Peninsula, just north of Japan, it observed the belching smoke plume of the Klyuchevskaya volcano. The September 1994 explosion of this andesitic volcano shot smoke and ash 36,949 feet (11,262 m) into the atmosphere. Winds carried this debris over 640 miles (1,030 kilometers). Air traffic had to fly longer routes to avoid the cloud of ash.*

Klyuchevskaya is one of a group of twenty volcanoes along the peninsula, situated on the Pacific "Ring of Fire." These volcanoes erupt, on average, three to five times each year.

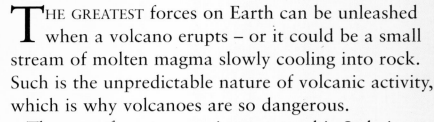

Strato volcanoes, formed by explosive andesitic magma, can be found in the Pacific's "Ring of Fire."

Shield volcanoes are less explosive than strato volcanoes and have the gently spreading slopes typical of Hawaiian volcanoes.

The shockwave can easily be seen around the volcano's slopes. Within the blast area, all the trees had fallen in the same direction.

APRIL, 1980
BEFORE

WHEN WASHINGTON BLEW ITS TOP

On the morning of May 18, 1980, Mount St. Helens, in the state of Washington, erupted. It was the first volcanic eruption in the continental United States in over 60 years. The volcano's summit collapsed, its sides burst outward triggering landslides, and a searingly hot ash cloud shot upward almost 12 miles (19 km). Within two weeks, this ash cloud had encircled Earth.

During the eruption, Mount St. Helens ejected 1 cubic mile (4 cubic kilometers) of airborne debris and lost 1,300 feet (396 m) of its original height. Sadly, eight geological observers lost their lives after being caught in the blast.

The mountain first exploded sideways, bulging outward. The force was the equivalent of a 10 megaton bomb – 500 times more deadly than the bomb that destroyed Hiroshima in 1945.

MAY 18, 1980
DURING

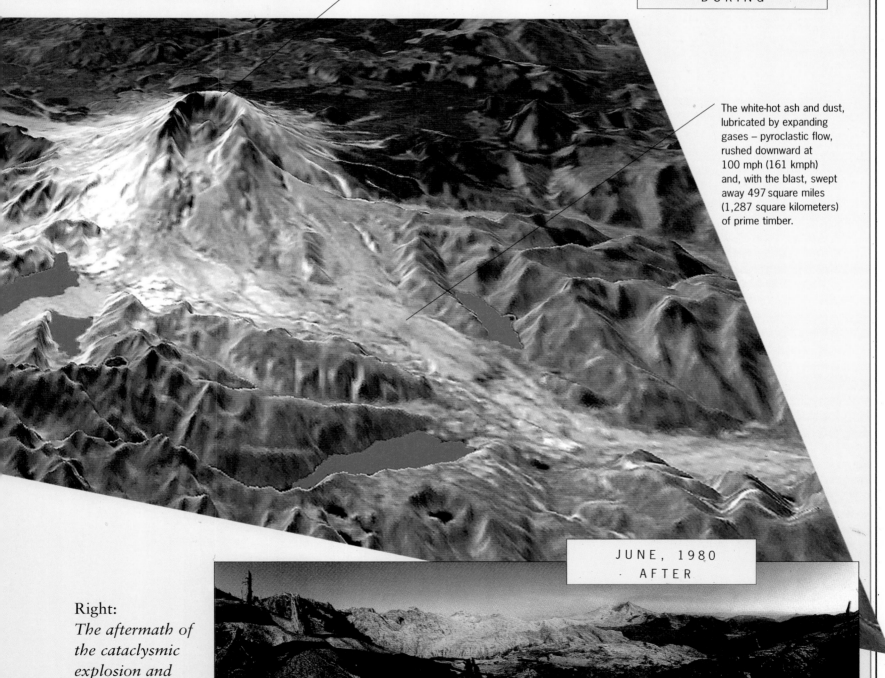

The white-hot ash and dust, lubricated by expanding gases – pyroclastic flow, rushed downward at 100 mph (161 kmph) and, with the blast, swept away 497 square miles (1,287 square kilometers) of prime timber.

JUNE, 1980
AFTER

Right:
The aftermath of the cataclysmic explosion and blast wave.

Spreading Rifts

See also:
- **Earth Movements** p. 16
- **Moving Plates** p. 18
- **Volcano!** p. 20
- **Building Mountains** p. 24

Below:
The western coastline of Africa matches the eastern edge of South America, from which it broke away 120 million years ago.

NEW PLATES form as molten rock from Earth's interior wells up along cracks and solidifies. This activity usually occurs under the sea, producing ocean ridges. Sometimes, however, it occurs beneath a continent, causing the landmass to split and break apart, which is what is happening to Africa.

A satellite photograph clearly shows the third crack in the African Plate – a string of underwater volcanoes, and the volcanic belt of the Cameroons.

OUT OF AFRICA

When Pangaea broke up into today's continents, it split along rifts. Africa is proof. Its coastlines form a jigsaw fit with those of the continents from which it split. What's more, Africa is still splitting, and the Rift Valley system, which stretches from the Red Sea down to Mozambique, shows where.

A rift usually starts as a rise in Earth's crust from which three cracks radiate. Two cracks develop the main rift movement, while the third crack is less active.

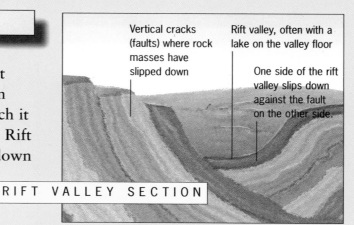

Vertical cracks (faults) where rock masses have slipped down

Rift valley, often with a lake on the valley floor

One side of the rift valley slips down against the fault on the other side.

RIFT VALLEY SECTION

Below:
The floor of the Rift Valley in Ethiopia (the Afar Triangle) matches the coastline of Yemen to the northeast.

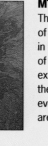

RED SEA RIFT
The opposite shores of the Red Sea match each other. They overlap only in the area of the Afar Triangle, where three cracks diverge.

MT. KENYA
This volcano is one of many volcanoes in the area, most of which are now extinct. Some of them have glaciers, even though they are on the equator.

RIFT LAKES
The great lakes that can be seen from space mark the Great Rift Valley in East Africa. They are the deepest lakes on the continent.

MADAGASCAR
This large island was once joined to Africa. It is now moving slowly toward India.

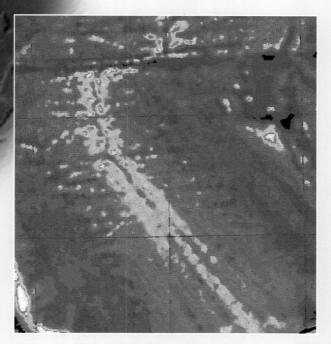

UNDERSEA BACKBONE

New plates are constantly being created along underwater ocean ridges. Molten rock, known as magma, wells to the surface along a rift and solidifies, forming mountains running parallel to the ridge. This rock then pulls apart and forms another rift, and more magma wells up and solidifies. Over the years, the rock builds up to form plates. The plates then move away from each other. The youngest part of the plate is closest to the rift; the oldest part is the furthest away.

Left:
Parallel mountain ridges along each side of the rift down the center of the Mid-Atlantic Ridge show where new crust is deposited.

Building Mountains

See also:
- **Earth Movements** *p. 16*
- **Moving Plates** *p. 18*
- **Volcano!** *p. 20*
- **Spreading Rifts** *p. 22*

WHEN TWO continental plates collide, it is like a traffic accident, but, instead of lasting for a few fractions of a second, the collision takes place over millions of years. The stresses and strains are enormous, and the forces have to escape in the only direction possible – upward. This is the way mountains are born.

FOUR BASIC TYPES OF MOUNTAINS

FOLDED

FAULT-BLOCK

VOLCANIC

DOME

Left:
This spiky profile is a young mountain. The most youthful rock lies at the top of the peak. A mere 50 million years ago, these rocks would have been mud and sand at the bottom of the sea. This peak is in the French Alps near the Italian border.

Mountain shapes are of distinct types. All of them have been formed by the actions of heat and pressure and have been weathered by wind and water.

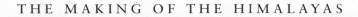

THE MAKING OF THE HIMALAYAS

About 165 million years ago, the Indian-Australian plate started to move northward toward the central Asian plate. As it hit the older and harder rocks, parts of the younger Indian Plate rose up and over the Asian Plate. At the same time, parts of it were pushed down into Earth's crust.

Today, the Himalayas are still rising, more than a quarter of an inch (0.6 cm) a year. In a million years, they could be 16,000 feet (4,877 m) higher – even allowing for some weathering.

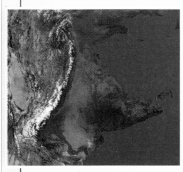

Above:
This view of the Indian subcontinent is from an orbiting satellite.

TIBETAN PLATEAU

Away from the point of impact, the rocks are crumpled up into hills.

"Young" mountains arise at the point of impact.

The thinner oceanic crust dives under the older, harder continental crust and melts to form new rocks hundreds of miles (km) below Earth's surface.

At the point of impact, rocks slip and slide under great pressure, causing heat to build up and the rock to metamorphose, or change, into new rock types. At this point, an earthquake might also occur.

Direction of movement

Oceanic crust is not as strong as the continental crust with which it collides.

The Himalayan mountains contain most of the world's peaks that are higher than 25,000 feet (7,620 m).

Mt. Everest, the world's highest point, rises 29,118 feet (8,875 m) above sea level.

INDIAN SUBCONTINENT

YOUNG AND OLD

"YOUNG" MOUNTAINS
Mountains with shapes that are sharp and jagged are called "young." This is Mount Everest.

"OLD" MOUNTAINS
The action of natural weathering gradually wears down the sharp edges of the rocks so they take on a rounded look. At this point, they become known as "old" mountains, like these in central Asia.

This three-dimensional computer model of India shows the Himalayan range in exaggerated perspective to emphasize the massive collision of the two plate boundaries that created the Himalayas. Compare it with the inset picture (opposite, far left).

Shake, Rattle, and Roll

See also:
- **Earth Movements** *p. 16*
- **Moving Plates** *p. 18*
- **Volcano!** *p. 20*
- **Spreading Rifts** *p. 22*

*Right and far right:
The San Andreas Fault,
shown as it appears a
few thousand feet
(about a thousand
meters) above the
Mojave Desert, at
some points bisects
highways and roads.*

EARTHQUAKES ARE, perhaps, the most deadly of all the catastrophes that can strike the human race. Over one million quakes shake the earth every year, but most of them are hardly ever felt.

When two layers of moving rock stick, instead of slide, forces build up, and, eventually, the energy is released with explosive power. The point at which this release occurs is called the "epicenter." Energy flows out from the epicenter like ripples on a pond after a stone has been thrown into it. The energy waves, which take different forms, can travel through the rock in seconds. The 1989 earthquake in San Francisco shook an area of 621 square miles (1,608 sq km), from southern Oregon to Los Angeles.

Earthquake epicenter   Landers township   Main fault lines

Above:
*On June 28, 1992, Landers township, in
California, was shaken by an earthquake of
7.3 magnitude. This computer enhancement
shows shock waves rippling outward from
the quake's epicenter.*

THE "BIG ONE"

For almost a century, Californians have been living in dread of the "Big One," an earthquake that will match the 7.7 magnitude shock that toppled San Francisco in 1906. The quake of 1989 in Northern California suggested that all would be far from well when the next large tremor strikes. Experts have warned that, when the time comes for another tremor, it will be preceded by a "seismic silence." Reliable earthquake prediction is still a long way off.

In some earthquake-prone countries, such as Italy and Turkey, new construction must be of an "earthquake-

THE FAULT LIES IN THE GROUND

The kinds of faults found in rock strata are each as deadly as the others. Coupled with the wavelike action of seismic shocks, it is little wonder that the earth shakes and twists.

Strike-slip fault

Normal fault

Reverse fault

SAN FRANCISCO
1906

SAN FRANCISCO
1989

SAN FRANCISCO
Much of the destruction in the 1989 earthquake was to structures built on land reclaimed after the 1906 earthquake.

SAN ANDREAS FAULT
The fault line can be seen clearly from space as it crosses San Francisco Bay. On the far left of this picture, the fault line is particularly visible just above the white-shored cape known as Point Reyes National Seashore.

proof" standard. Reinforced concrete is now suspect because, under certain conditions, it can crumble. In the United States, engineers are experimenting with frameworks that sway rather than crack, rubber cushions to separate buildings from the ground, and computer-controlled pistons to counteract an earthquake's movement.

Fire almost inevitably follows an earthquake, so emergency services plan accordingly.

The Rock Story

See also:
- **Volcano!** p. 20
- **Spreading Rifts** p. 22
- **Rivers** p. 38
- **. . . and Deltas** p. 42

A s OLD as the hills – Earth's crust is thought to be indestructible. In fact, however, the rocks that make up hills and mountains are constantly being broken down and rebuilt.

They might be rebuilt after being melted and resolidified; they might be compressed and "cooked" into completely new types of rocks; or they might be broken down by erosion and fused together into different rock types. The constant renewing of Earth's surface is known as the rock cycle.

Above:
The Grand Canyon, carved by the Colorado River, is 217 miles (349 km) long. Erosion over five to ten million years has laid bare the rock's geological history in a layer more than 1 mile (1.6 km) deep.

Below:
These rock columns in Northern Ireland are made of solidified lava that came from a now extinct basaltic volcano. Basalt is an igneous rock.

HOW ROCKS ARE FORMED

Rocks are gradually broken down by weathering and erosion. The debris is slowly washed away and piles up to form a deep layer of sediment. Through time, this layer of sediment is compressed and compacted by the weight of additional layers. Water passing through the sediment deposits minerals between the rock particles, cementing the particles into a solid mass.

The end result is sedimentary rock, one of three kinds of rocks. Sedimentary rock is formed in horizontal layers, called strata. The strata become visible when the rock is exposed by river erosion, as in the Grand Canyon, or when hills formed of sedimentary rocks, like the Appalachians, are worn away.

The other two kinds of rocks are igneous rock – formed from magma – and metamorphic rock – shaped by Earth's forces from pre-existing rock.

Metamorphic rock is created when rock buried deep inside a mountain chain is compressed and heated, perhaps through the movement of tectonic plates. The mineral crystals in the rock break down and realign to create new rocks with a different texture. Marble, shale, and schist are metamorphic rocks.

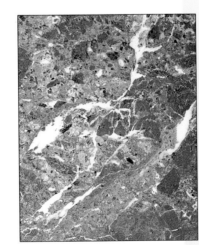

Right :
Marble is an example of metamorphic rock. This rock was once sedimentary limestone, until pressure and heat altered it. The many beautiful colors of marble come from impurities in the original limestone.

BORN IN FIRE

The molten material, or magma, within Earth may be squeezed to the surface and erupt through volcanoes or ooze out onto the ocean floor. The magma will cool and solidify into a fine-grained, extrusive igneous rock. If the magma cools and solidifies before it reaches the surface, it produces an intrusive igneous rock, such as granite. Granite is coarse-grained, with big crystals of minerals in it.

SANDS OF TIME

The different types of sedimentary rock, along with the structures and fossils embedded in them, help us understand the history of Earth.

ROCK TYPES
Rock fragments, such as the rounded pebbles of this shingle beach, become a coarse sedimentary rock known as conglomerate. Sand forms sandstone. Silts and mud create siltstone and shale. Chemical deposits on the seafloor form limestone.

SEDIMENTARY STRUCTURES
Silt dried by the Sun shrivels, forming cracks that can be preserved in siltstone. Ripples in shore sand and pits formed by rainfall can also be preserved. They are witnesses to ancient climates.

LIFE OF THE PAST
The remains of animals, birds, and plants that lived and died when layers of sediment were being deposited were often buried and preserved as fossils. With the evidence these fossils provide, we can plot the history of life on Earth.

Right :
A massive amount of silt and sand is transported by rivers, then deposited in estuaries and deltas, like the Mekong delta in Vietnam.

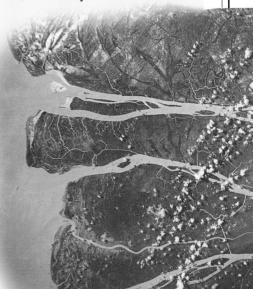

Fallen Stars

See also:
- **Earth in Space** p. 12
- **Volcano!** p. 20
- **Building Mountains** p. 24
- **Shake, Rattle, and Roll** p. 26

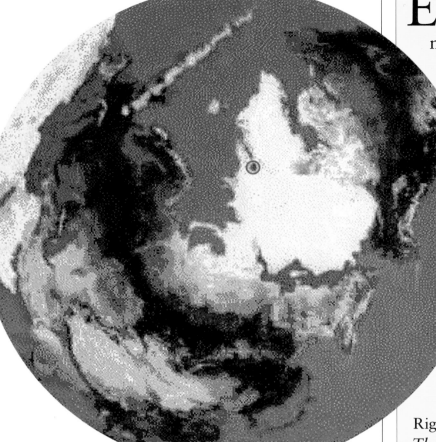

EARTH HAS been bombarded by rocky debris from space, in the form of comets and meteorites, ever since the planet was formed. Most meteorites burn up in the atmosphere, but a few are large enough to reach the ground. In recent years, there have been a few "near misses," such as when the comet Shoemaker-Levy tore itself apart going around Jupiter in 1994. What would be the effect on Earth of such a strike? Statistically, it is only a matter of time before another comet threatens our planet.

Above:
This satellite view shows the sooty impact site of a possible comet landing on Greenland in December 1997. Comets are made of "dirty snow" and ice, while meteorites are solid rock.

Right:
The crater at Manicouagan in Quebec, Canada, is 47 miles (76 km) wide and is thought to be 210 million years old.
The meteorite struck the ancient rock of the Canadian Shield, so the crater has not been destroyed by plate movement.

YUCATAN IMPACT SITE

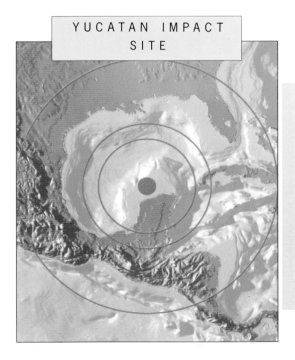

Radins of iridium deposit mark the extent of asteroid impact.

THE BIGGEST HIT YET?

Sixty-five million years ago, something wiped out the dinosaurs and most other life on Earth. The culprit was probably a vast meteorite that landed in Chicxulub, Mexico, forming a crater 110 miles (177 km) in diameter. The dust and gases sent high into the atmosphere would have changed the climate for a long time, making Earth cold and dark. Plants could not have survived, and animals would have starved to death.

HOW TO MAKE AN IMPRESSION

A meteorite rips into the surface of Earth with explosive impact, melting a large crater and blasting out debris. Craters on the Moon look similar.

1 The meteorite enters at an angle, so it is not deflected by Earth's atmosphere.

2 Rocky "ejecta" is blasted out of the crater made by the meteorite. The heat of the impact fuses and transforms rocks over the whole collision area.

3 A high-profiled edge is formed around the crater. Over time, this edge erodes away.

Dust settles in the hole made by the impact of the meteorite. A mountain in the center forms from rock pulled up by the explosion.

Below:
Meteor Crater in Arizona was made about 50,000 years ago. It is more than 570 feet (174 m) deep and about three quarters of a mile (1.2 km) in diameter. An impact like this on a city is unimaginable.

Squashed Forests

See also:
• . . . **Lakes** p. 40
• . . . **and Deltas** p. 42
• **Changing Coasts** p. 62

Below:
The swamp forests of the coal ages were similar to the modern delta swamps of the equatorial rain forest.

COAL IS fossilized plant material. For millions of years, swamp forests on Earth absorbed the energy of the Sun and the carbon dioxide of the atmosphere as they grew. When the trees died, they were buried by other plant material and, due to the lack of oxygen, did not rot. After millions of years of compression, the carbon in this material turned into coal. Today, when we burn coal, we release the energy stored all those millions of years ago.

Left:
This fossil leaf is typical of the plants that formed the Carboniferous period forest.

Vegetation dies and sinks into muddy swamp water. Layers of this organic debris build up over centuries.

HOW A SWAMP BECOMES COAL

A layer of dead plant material is buried in river sand. Over millions of years, this layer is compressed as other layers form on top of it. As the sand turns into sandstone, the plant material loses much of its hydrogen and oxygen, and the carbon becomes more condensed. The greater the proportion of carbon, the higher the grade of coal.

Peat forms as dead vegetation is compressed and loses its moisture.

COAL IN NORTH AMERICA

Most of the world's coal was formed during the Carboniferous period, about 300 million years ago. At this time, newly formed mountain ranges were eroding, spreading sediment across shallow seas, which produced large areas of delta that became covered with swamp forests.

Coal from the Carboniferous period is found in eastern North America, in Pennsylvania and Ohio. Lignite, which is coal from the Permian period, is found in the Great Plains and further west, on into the Rockies.

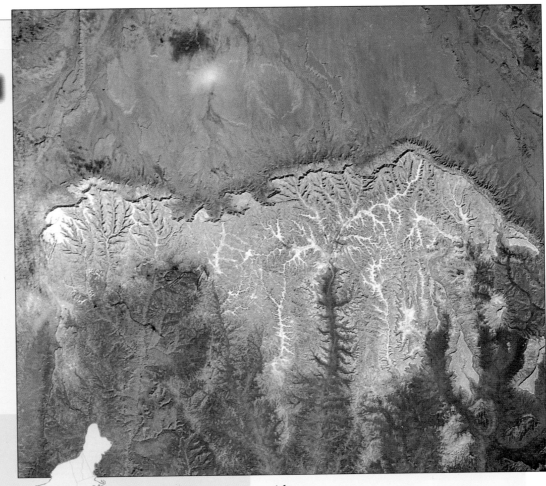

Above:
Many coalfields, such as Black Mesa in the Arizona Desert of the United States, formed in the more recent Permian period. Permian coal is a lower grade coal.

Coalfields close to the surface can be mined by the open pit method.

COAL ZONES IN THE USA

Key:
Carboniferous outcrops ■

Permian outcrops ▫

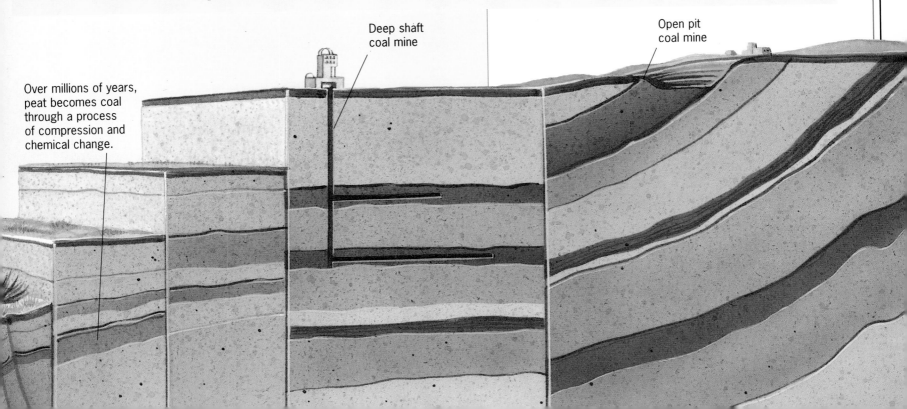

Over millions of years, peat becomes coal through a process of compression and chemical change.

Deep shaft coal mine

Open pit coal mine

Black Gold

See also:
- ... **Lakes** p. 40
- ... **and Deltas** p. 42
- **Changing Coasts** p. 62

Above:
Oil and gas move through porous rocks, usually floating upward through the groundwater. They are lost at the surface, unless they are caught in rock structures called traps. The Zagros Mountains of Iran (above) and other areas of the Middle East are full of these traps, giving rise to the great oil industries of those areas.

Left:
These oil refinery tanks and pipelines are in Saudi Arabia.

MUCH OF today's economy is based on oil. Oil is used as both a fuel and a power source, and it is also a valuable raw material. Many kinds of plastics are made from oil.

Like coal, oil is a fossil fuel. It forms from the remains of tiny sea creatures buried on the ocean floor under layers of sediment, where lack of oxygen prevents the normal process of decay. Bacterial action and heat from within Earth break down these substances into a series of carbon compounds trapped in underground rock. These carbon compounds are the raw materials that form gas and oil. When the gas and oil collect in large pockets underground, they can be extracted.

THE CLUE OF THE SALT DOMES

Oil traps are usually found where rocks are buckled upward in curved layers. Oil can gather beneath a layer, like air in an upside-down cup in a sinkful of water. The crumpled, oilbearing rocks of the Arabian Gulf have many traps, including those formed by "salt domes."

Since layers of salt are lighter than other rocks, they tend to rise through the other rock layers, twisting those layers up as they go. These twisted rock beds form ideal traps, so oil geologists look for layers like these.

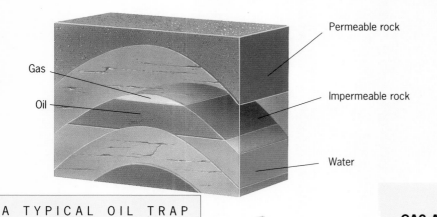

Permeable rock

Gas

Oil

Impermeable rock

Water

A TYPICAL OIL TRAP

Main concentrations of oil

GAS AND OIL IN THE NORTH SEA
The North Sea, between Great Britain and Europe, contains many oil traps. Gas deposits are exploited in the southern North Sea, but they come from the break-down of coal deposits, not from oil.

NORTH SEA

Main gas production areas

Main gas pipelines

Left:
Because of the depth and fierce currents of the North Sea, construction techniques for gas and oil platforms are highly developed.

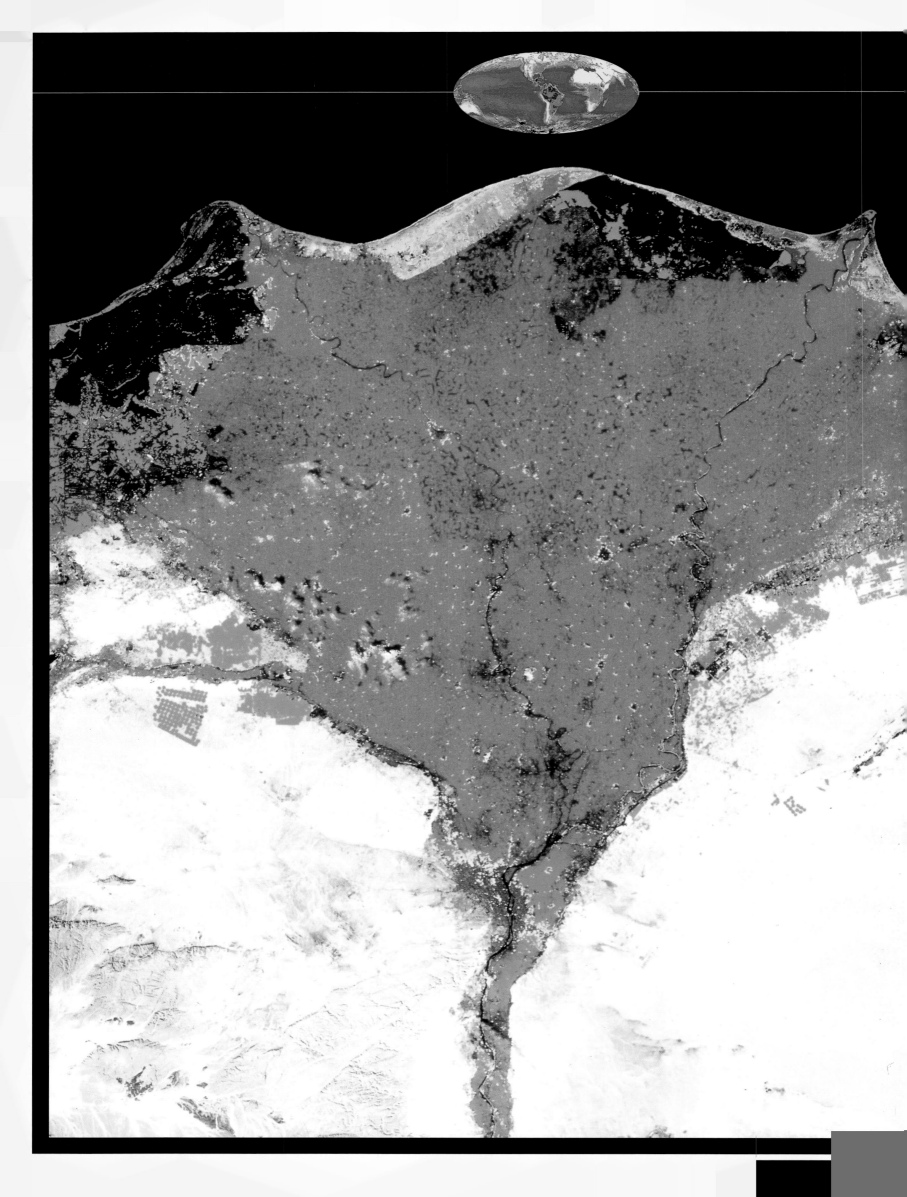

PART TWO

Earth in Action

Earth changes before our eyes as water carves out channels through and under the ground, and desert sands shift in the wind.

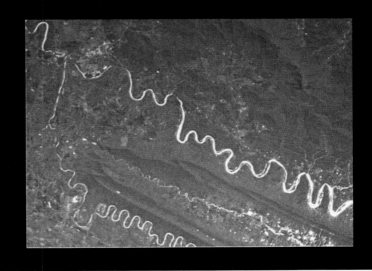

Rivers

See also:
- . . . **Lakes** p. 40
- . . . **and Deltas** p. 42
- **Eroding Earth** p. 44
- **Changing Coasts** p. 62

Below:
Rivers can modify the landscape through the processes of erosion and deposition. Typically, a river goes through three stages: the first is erosion, the third is deposition, and the second is a balance between the two, as shown in these photographs.

RIVERS ARE an essential part of the water cycle on Earth. The Sun evaporates water from the surfaces of the oceans. The water vapor is then blown by winds over the continents.

When the atmosphere changes in pressure or in temperature, the water vapor condenses into clouds and falls as rain or snow. Water falling on the land runs together and eventually produces rivers that carry the water back to the oceans. The water cycle continues every second of every day and has done so for millions of years.

FIRST STAGE

SECOND STAGE

RIVER VALLEY
After passing through its first stage, a river's energy is reduced. It can still erode a valley, but most of the erosion takes place at the sides, and the valley tends to be broad. This is the Shenandoah River in Virginia.

MOUNTAIN STREAM
A swiftly flowing stream in the Alps is full of energy as it rushes down the mountainside, eroding its bed into a deep ravine. The eroded rock is picked up and carried along, adding to the erosive force.

FLOOD PLAIN
As the current slackens, eroded material falls to the riverbed, and soil and mud are laid on the valley floor. When the river floods, it deposits whole sheets of sediment, creating a flat-bottomed valley over which the river meanders.

RIVER STAGES AND SHAPES

In a river's first stage, when it runs in a deep, V-shaped gorge, there is no depositing of material, only erosion.

In the second stage, when the river runs across layers of its own sediment, it is deeper on the outside curves, where the current is faster. As it gradually erodes the outside curves and deposits sediment on the inside, the river constantly changes its course.

In the third stage, so much sediment is deposited that the river may be above the level of the plain, held back by levees – banks of sediment deposited during floods.

FIRST STAGE PROFILE

SECOND STAGE PROFILE

THIRD STAGE PROFILE

THIRD STAGE

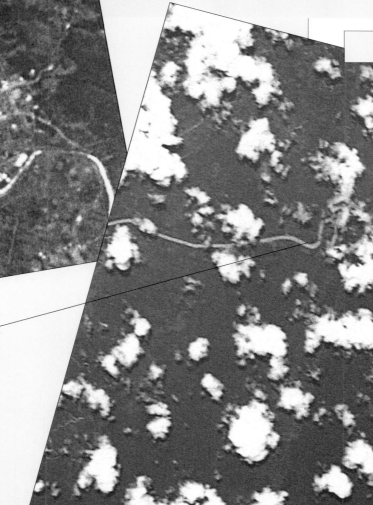

SPENT POWER
In the last stage of its life, the river has lost most of its power. It slowly meanders across the land in great loops, often cut off as oxbow lakes. Mud and silt are deposited on the flood plain or near the river's mouth, as on the coastal plain of Sarawak, shown here.

. . . Lakes

See also:
- **Volcano!** p. 20
- **Spreading Rifts** p. 22
- **Rivers** p. 38
- **. . . and Deltas** p. 42

Below:

As passing glaciers melted, lakes formed in hollows made deeper by the weight of the ice. Glaciers also deposited rocky material (moraine), forming dams that held back the water from the melting ice. The Great Lakes of North America are examples of lakes formed by glacial action.

THERE ARE probably more lakes on Earth's surface now than at any other time in its history. The three main kinds of lakes are: lakes scooped out by glaciers; lakes formed in hollows produced by the movements of Earth, such as rift valley lakes; and lakes formed when a river flows into an inland basin. There are also artificial lakes, formed when a river is dammed or when lagoons are cut off from the sea. Most lakes are freshwater, but some accumulate minerals and may become saltier than the sea.

PRESENT DAY

Below:

Over time, the margins of lakes become overgrown with vegetation that gradually encroaches on the water until the lake becomes a swamp, or even covered over entirely.

Lake Erie was once the most polluted body of water in the world, because of industrial effluent flowing into it. Now, with strict environmental controls, the water is clear again.

Lake Michigan

Hollows filled with water

11,000 YEARS AGO
Eroded hollows filled with water as glacier ice began to melt. Water from the original Lake Michigan flowed southward to the Mississippi River.

11,000 YEARS AGO

LAKES FROM EARTH MOVEMENTS

Lake Baikal in Siberia is a typical rift valley lake. The rift valley was formed by the plate movements that are slowly tearing Asia apart. As the valley has formed over the last 50 million years, it has filled with water, making Lake Baikal the oldest lake on Earth.

Other earth-movement lakes include the crater lakes of extinct volcanoes, where water has filled the caldera, the crater left after the explosion and collapse of the cone. Crater Lake in Oregon (USA) is a good example.

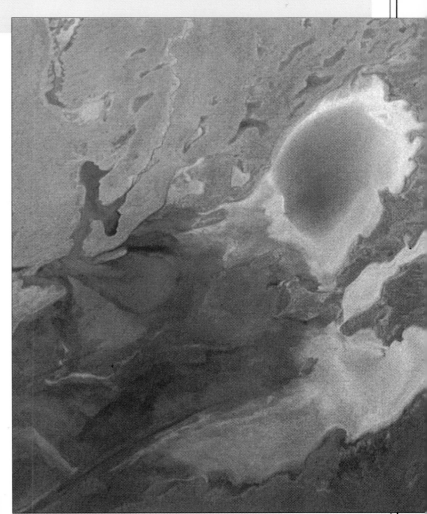

HOW THE LAKES BECAME GREAT

At the height of the last Ice Age, half of North America was covered with ice. As the ice sheet, with its embedded rubble and debris, advanced southward, it scoured existing lowlands and valleys, deepening and widening them into the basins now occupied by the Great Lakes. At the end of the Ice Age, those basins filled with water from the melted ice. Today's raised beaches show that the Great Lakes were, at certain times in the past, far more extensive than they are now. These lakes are estimated to contain about 20 percent of the world's freshwater.

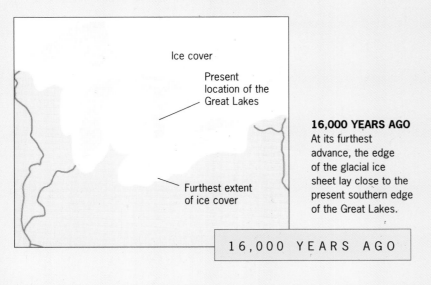

Ice cover

Present location of the Great Lakes

Furthest extent of ice cover

16,000 YEARS AGO
At its furthest advance, the edge of the glacial ice sheet lay close to the present southern edge of the Great Lakes.

16,000 YEARS AGO

AUSTRALIA'S GREAT SALT LAKE

In desert areas during the wet season, rivers from surrounding hills may flow into inland basins and form lakes.

During the dry season, all the water evaporates, leaving plains of salt. The example shown above is Lake Eyre in Southern Australia. Salt lakes also can be found in Death Valley, California.

... and Deltas

See also:
- **Rivers** p. 38
- **... Lakes** p. 40
- **Eroding Earth** p. 44
- **Changing Coasts** p. 62

Below:
The great sprawling mass of dark green in this photograph is the Okavango delta at the edge of the Kalahari Desert basin. Although most deltas are formed at the mouth of a river, where it flows into the sea, the Okavango is a rare example of an inland delta, built up during the rainy seasons.

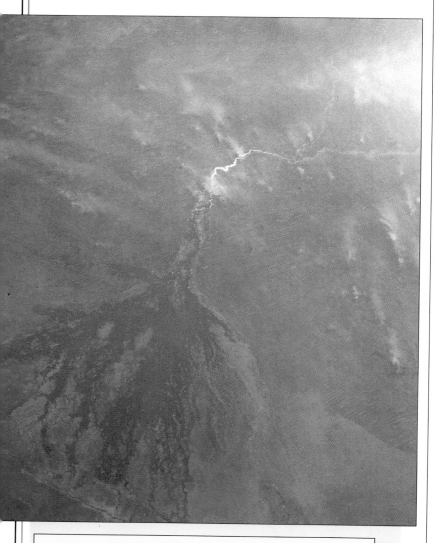

THE INLAND DELTA

In Botswana, in southern Africa, the Okavango River forms an inland delta as it spreads out at the edge of the vast, semi-arid Kalahari Desert. Its seasonal, watery fingers stretch out over 805 square miles (2,085 sq km).

During the rainy season, water flows into this delta and plant life flourishes. Grazing animals migrate there to feed, as a relief from the dry conditions in the surrounding desert plains.

As a river flows into the sea, it brings with it much of the sand and silt it has picked up on its journey. If there are no strong tides or currents to wash it away, this sediment sinks to the bottom, gradually building up a fan-shaped deposit. Over time, the river changes its course to find a way through and might split into many shifting channels, forming a delta that is commonly shaped like the Greek letter Δ (delta).

Because of their rich silt, deltas are very fertile and have always attracted human settlement. Cairo, New Orleans, and Calcutta all are cities built on deltas.

THE MAKING OF THE NILE DELTA

Five and a half million years ago, the Mediterranean Sea did not exist. The Nile River flowed from Africa to a low desert plain between North Africa and Europe. Over time, the river laid down a huge alluvial "fan" of sediment. Today, most of the eastern Mediterranean seafloor is made of this sediment.

With fertile silt and a constant water supply, the Nile delta has been cultivated throughout history. Its character, however, has changed. The number of irrigation ditches has increased, and the flow of the river is now controlled by the Aswan Dam. Such changes are starving the delta of new sediment and are causing the front of the delta to erode.

5.5 MILLION YEARS AGO

800,000 YEARS AGO

PRESENT DAY

Above:
The Nile delta can be seen clearly from space. In recent years, the delta has become clogged with plants, causing problems for the Egyptians about how best to manage this changing environment.

RIVER AND MAN

The Mississippi delta is a "bird's foot" delta. Its pattern is shaped by river channels forming levees (low mounds of sediment) that reach out into the waters of the Gulf of Mexico. Because the floor of the Gulf of Mexico is subsiding, much of the sediment carried out to sea is spreading over the seabed, leaving the levees to form the delta.

Today, the Mississippi River exits eastward, via New Orleans. If, however, humans had not intervened to maintain the existing channels, it would have swung south again by now.

Eroding Earth

See also:
- **Volcano!** *p. 20*
- **Spreading Rifts** *p. 22*
- **Rivers** *p. 38*
- **. . . and Deltas** *p. 42*

A s SOON as rocks are lifted above sea level, the forces of nature combine to wear them away in a process known as erosion. Erosion takes place when elements, such as wind, rain, ice, or sea waves, act on rocks to break them up and carry away the fragments.

Weathering – either physical, such as freezing and thawing or the growth of plant roots, or chemical, when chemicals in the atmosphere react with minerals in the rocks – also causes rocks to break apart or crumble.

Below:
The Dalmatian coastline in Slovenia consists of islands and inlets running parallel to the shore, formed by the eroded ridges and valleys of parallel mountain ranges. The limestone rocks have gradually been eroded and dissolved by water.

FORCES AT WORK

A TYPICAL CAVE SYSTEM

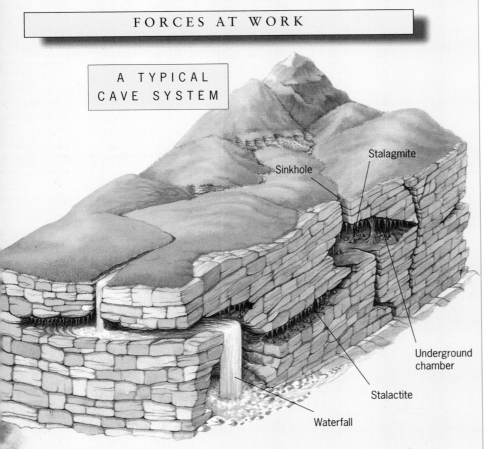

Sinkhole

Stalagmite

Underground chamber

Stalactite

Waterfall

Limestone is a soluble rock that is very vulnerable to chemical weathering. Its main component, calcite, is broken down by the acid in groundwater into calcium carbonate, which dissolves in the water. The end result is a "karst" landscape, named for a region in Slovenia where barren limestone is dissolved into hollows and cracks, and the rocks beneath are riddled with caves and caverns carved out by the water.

SPECTACULAR EFFECTS

A limestone cavern is shaped as the limestone is dissolved by acid in groundwater. The horizontal galleries that form along the water table can be left dry if the water table drops. Side caves are eroded along joints and bedding planes, where the rock is most vulnerable.

Right:
Water passing through limestone can build as well as destroy. Dissolved calcite in groundwater can be deposited on the walls and roofs of caves, forming spectacular stalagmites, going up, and stalactites, coming down.

LANDSLIDES AND WATER

The most dramatic form of erosion is caused by landslides that occur when a slope becomes unstable. Landslides can be triggered in several different ways.

Very often, human activities cause landslides. A landslide in Naples, in 1998, happened because there was no control on building, and too many houses were built on a slope that was not strong enough to support them.

In some areas, the soil on a slope becomes unstable when vegetation is removed, particularly when trees are cut down. Rainwater gradually loosens the soil until, eventually, a mass of mud slides downhill, often with disastrous results.

SOIL CREEP This slow erosion is caused by the gradual movement of soil and other particles downhill.

MUDSLIDES When trees are cut down on a slope, the loose soil mixes with water during a storm and slides downward.

SCREE The action of frost causes broken rocks to split away from a hillside and form a rubbly slope.

CLIFF SLUMPS A mass of solid rock cracks and slides downward along a curved surface.

Shifting Deserts

See also:
- **Polar Regions** *p. 48*
- **Frozen Earth** *p. 52*
- **Moving Bands** *p. 54*
- **El Niño** *p. 58*

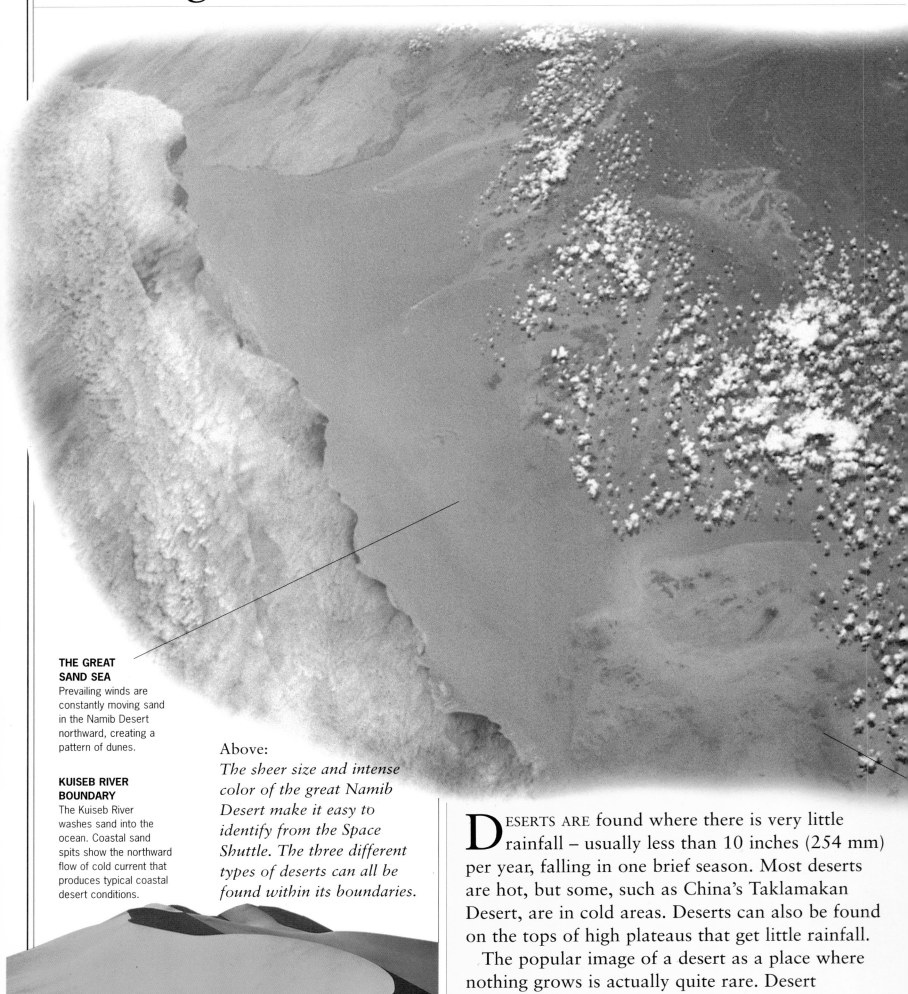

THE GREAT SAND SEA
Prevailing winds are constantly moving sand in the Namib Desert northward, creating a pattern of dunes.

KUISEB RIVER BOUNDARY
The Kuiseb River washes sand into the ocean. Coastal sand spits show the northward flow of cold current that produces typical coastal desert conditions.

Above:
The sheer size and intense color of the great Namib Desert make it easy to identify from the Space Shuttle. The three different types of deserts can all be found within its boundaries.

DESERTS ARE found where there is very little rainfall – usually less than 10 inches (254 mm) per year, falling in one brief season. Most deserts are hot, but some, such as China's Taklamakan Desert, are in cold areas. Deserts can also be found on the tops of high plateaus that get little rainfall.

The popular image of a desert as a place where nothing grows is actually quite rare. Desert vegetation can consist of very poor grassland or scrub and succulent plants, such as cacti.

SKELETON COAST

The Namib is a coastal desert, formed by cold sea currents flowing from the Antarctic. The cold sea cools the air above and causes it to descend, producing dry desert conditions because rain falls only from ascending air.

To the east, the Namib Desert blends into the Kalahari, a tropical desert. Warm air rises at the equator, dropping all of its moisture as rain and producing rain forest. As dry air drifts away from the equator, it cools and descends at the latitudes of the Tropics, producing the tropical desert belts.

DESERT ZONES

Tropical deserts form where dry air descends along the tropics of Cancer and Capricorn. These deserts include the Sahara and Mexican deserts along the Tropic of Cancer and the Kalahari and Australian deserts along the Tropic of Capricorn.

Continental deserts, such as the Gobi, are dry because of their distance from the sea. Coastal deserts, such as the Atacama and the Namib, form where cold ocean currents flow toward the equator.

Rain shadow deserts, such as the Mojave and Patagonian, lie in the shelter of mountains, where only dry air reaches them.

Key:

Tropical

Continental

Rain shadow

ROCKY AND STONY DESERTS

The Namib Desert, in southern Africa, is an example of all three types of deserts. It not only has sand but also contains stretches of stony desert pavement and exposed bedrock with little soil.

THREE TYPES OF DESERTS

Within the various desert zones, there are three different types of deserts. Each type has its own distinctive landforms. Wind is an important agent in the shaping of many desert landforms.

SAND DESERT
The sand sea is the most familiar type of desert. Wind erosion reduces exposed rocks to sand, which is blown along slowly in low hills called dunes.

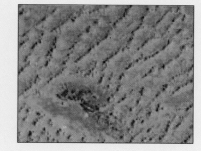

STONY DESERT
A stony desert has a surface, or pavement, of wind-polished stones. The pavement might consist of only a crust covering a layer of finer dust.

ROCKY DESERT
Dry desert conditions mean few plants can grow, and no soil can form. So the bedrock of the landscape is exposed and eroded.

DESERT AREAS OF THE WORLD

60°N

Turkmenistan

Gobi

Mojave

Iran

Chihuahua

30° N

Sahara

Arabian

Thar

Somalia

Equator

Australian

Atacama

Namib

Kalahari

30°S

Monte

Patagonian

60°S

Polar Regions

See also:
- **Volcano!** *p. 20*
- **Spreading Rifts** *p. 22*
- **Rivers of Ice** *p. 50*
- **Holes in the Sky** *p. 76*

Below and right:
These satellite images show the two great masses of the Arctic (below) and Antarctica (right). The Arctic is mainly frozen sea. Antarctica is a landmass covered with an ice sheet.

THE TWO great masses of ice at either end of the planet hold well over 90 percent of the world's freshwater supply. Each year, as Earth gets warmer, the ice shrinks and the oceans get deeper. In Antarctica, the average thickness of the ice is 6,500 feet (1,980 m). In the Arctic, sea ice is 10 to 16 feet (3 to 5 m) thick.

There are no volcanoes in the Arctic, but five active ones have been found in Antarctica.

Below:
Arctic icebergs float away into the North Atlantic Ocean. These icebergs are sharply shaped, unlike their flat-topped Antarctic cousins.

FIVE VARIETIES OF ICE

FRAZIL ICE

GREASE ICE

PANCAKE ICE

SEA-ICE SHEETS

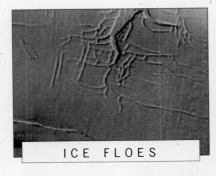
ICE FLOES

Scientists have recognized five different forms of ice in the polar regions. The Arctic has a more placid sea, and only four of the five types (not frazil ice) have been found there.

FRAZIL ICE
Water that freezes fast, causing chaotic crystal growth, shows evidence of stormy seas.

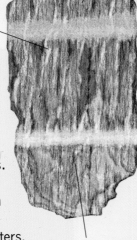

AN ICY SLIVER
Unlike Arctic ice, which is usually only one layer, Antarctic ice has two distinct layers. The base layer, called congelation ice, is associated with calm, still waters.

Congelation ice

As icebergs separate from ice shelves, they can break away in a spectacular manner. This iceberg (below), photographed from a height of 352 miles (566 km), measured 1,949 square miles (5,048 sq km), which is larger than the state of Rhode Island.

ALPHA 24,
SOUTH ATLANTIC

The visible size of an iceberg is deceptive because over two-thirds of it lies underwater. Perhaps the most famous iceberg was the one hit by the *Titanic* in 1912; over 1,500 people died.

ICEBERGS IN THE MAKING

Norwegian polar explorer, Roald Amundsen, once camped on the Ross Ice Shelf of Antarctica. He thought the shelf was firm ground, but in recent years, it has been breaking up. Some experts attribute this to pressure caused by a fault deep under the landmass.

THE SHELF AT REST
This series of images, photographed by a U.S. defense satellite over a period of three years, shows the gradual disintegration of the Ross Ice Shelf on the continent of Antarctica.

NOVEMBER 1986

CRACKS APPEAR
Almost a year after the first picture was taken, a long diagonal crack appeared at the seaward edge of the shelf. A second crack, immediately below the long crack, also shows signs of breaking away.

OCTOBER 1987

BREAKAWAY
A large chunk of ice has broken free and floated away, drifting into the middle of the image. Snowfalls have covered the second crack, which now shows signs of lengthening. It, too, will break free of the main ice mass.

DECEMBER 1988

Rivers of Ice

See also:
- **Building Mountains** *p. 24*
- . . . **Lakes** *p. 40*
- **Polar Regions** *p. 48*
- **Changing Coasts** *p. 62*

Below:
This image from a Landsat satellite shows part of the Byrd Glacier in Antarctica. The ice floe, together with dark streaks of rocky debris, called moraine, can be seen oozing out between the mountain ranges.

GLACIERS ARE "the plows of Earth." The raw power they harness rips up the surface beneath and crumbles it into powdered rock. Glaciers shape the land over which they move by carving out huge valleys over millions of years. They can transport rock boulders weighing hundreds of tons and deposit them, as the glacier slowly melts, many miles away. Although glaciers are so powerful, most of them move less than 3 feet (1 m) a year. These rivers of ice can be 1,000 feet (300 m) wide and many miles (km) long. They cover almost 11 percent of the world's land surface.

WHERE TO FIND ICE

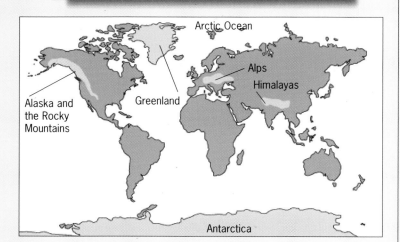

Arctic Ocean

Alps

Himalayas

Greenland

Alaska and
the Rocky
Mountains

Antarctica

Over 6 million square miles (15.5 million sq km) of Earth are permanently covered with ice, including Arctic Sea ice, Antarctic and Greenland ice sheets, ice caps, ice shelves, and high-altitude glaciers.

THE ANATOMY OF A GLACIER

Snow gathers in a hollow, or cirque, at the top of a mountain. As the snow builds up, it spills over and slowly flows down like a river. Crevasses, or cracks, form where the angle of the slope changes. Rocky debris, or moraine, is deposited at the sides and foot.

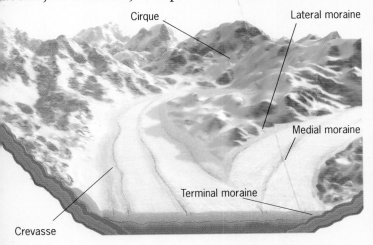

Cirque

Lateral moraine

Medial moraine

Terminal moraine

Crevasse

Above:
A sinister puff of snow can herald the onset of an avalanche, signaling death and destruction within moments.

Left:
In this view from space, the Cook Glacier on New Zealand's South Island shows many of its classic glacial landscape features.

AVALANCHE!

One of the worst avalanches of recent years occurred in Peru in 1962 when 3 million tons of debris from the glacial ice mass above Mt. Huascaran fell onto the slope of the main glacier and cascaded down onto villages in the valley below. This avalanche of rock, ice, and mud, already about 45 feet (14 m) high, gathered more debris as it descended into the valley. When its journey ended, 2 minutes later, 2,400 people were dead.

Frozen Earth

See also:
- **Polar Regions** p. 48
- **Rivers of Ice** p. 50
- **Moving Bands** p. 54

Above and right:
These two views of the Canadian tundra, from a Landsat orbiter (above) *and from the Space Shuttle* (right), *convey the bleakness of this wasteland.*

Below:
This image of the great landmass of Asia shows the tundra regions in summer. Reindeer and musk ox find enough mosses, grasses, and lichens to eat during the summer, but they migrate south to the forests in winter.

I{N THE} Northern Hemisphere, the last vegetation zone after the tree line and before the ice cap is known as tundra. In the Southern Hemisphere, only the southern tip of South America has tundra. Antarctica is almost totally covered with ice.

More than half of the year, tundra plains are covered with snow and ice. During short, cool summers, the snow and ice melt, but the water cannot drain away, so great areas of lake, pond, and marsh develop.

ICE POWER

There is a permanently frozen layer of soil, called permafrost, at tundra latitudes. In Siberia and Canada, the permafrost can be as deep as 1,650 feet (500 m). Because it remains frozen even in summer, when surface soil thaws, meltwater cannot drain away through it. Repeated freezing and thawing of surface soil creates patterned ground, including stone polygons and low hills, known as pingos. A pingo is a mound of earth with a core of ice that is constantly enlarging from below, stressing and cracking the crust of soil on top.

Above:
Repeated freezing and thawing on the tundra breaks topsoil into polygons, as shown here at Spitzbergen.

PERMAFROST SLICE

Surface soil thaws in the summer.

Permafrost is permanently frozen soil.

BOUNDARIES IN ICE

There are no tall trees on the tundra, and, because the ground is frozen most of the year, it has a very short growing season. Mosses, lichens, and grasses are the only vegetation that appears in summer. The few trees that survive are stunted; they cannot grow in the long, dark winter with its icy winds. As the tundra approaches the polar region, trees disappear entirely.

Limit of the tree line around the northern polar region

Right:
Tombstone Valley in the Yukon, in Alaska, is set alight by autumn colors. For a few short weeks, the scrub, plants, and lichen transform the tundra wilderness into a technicolor blaze.

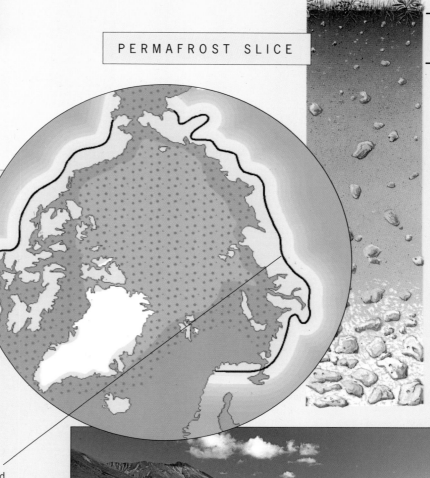

Moving Bands

See also:
• . . . **Lakes** p. 40   • **Shifting Deserts** p. 46
• . . . **and Deltas** p. 42

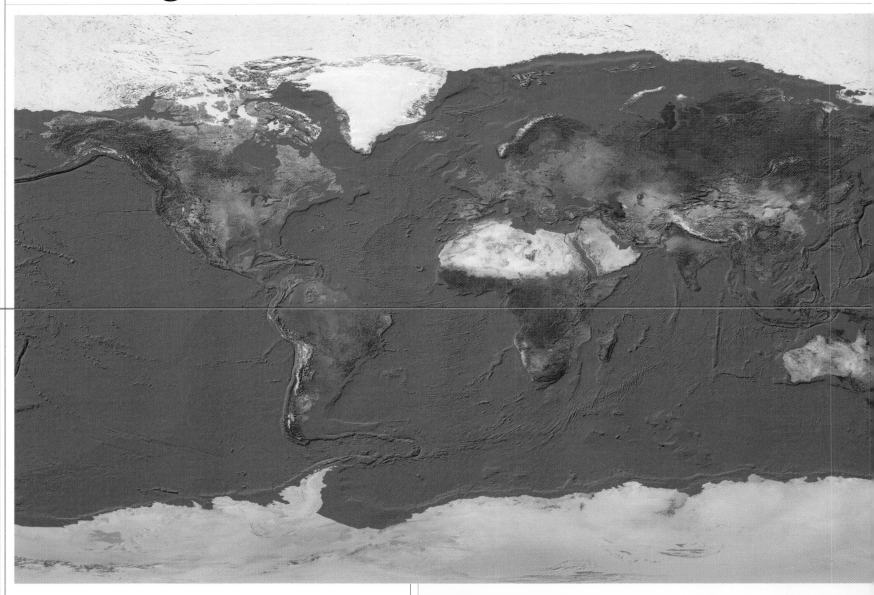

Above:
This composite image of Earth shows how vegetation and habitats form a mirror image north and south of the equator.

The NATURAL vegetation zones of Earth closely follow the climate zones, because plant life is very much controlled by climate. Hot and wet conditions, such as near the equator, produce forest. In seasonal dry conditions, grasses and grassy plains thrive, but not trees. In dry climates, only desert vegetation is found. Very cold climates produce forests of conifers, trees that can withstand freezing conditions and shake off heavy coverings of snow.

WHY THERE ARE SEASONS

Earth's axis is tilted at an angle to its orbit around the Sun, so, at one time of year, the North Pole is pointing toward the Sun, and it is summer in the Northern Hemisphere and winter in the Southern Hemisphere. Six months later, it is pointing away, and these seasons are reversed. At the start of each of these seasons, called the solstice, the Sun is at either its highest or lowest point in the sky.

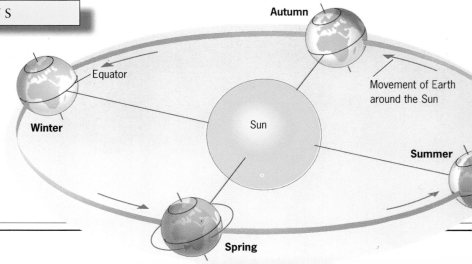

SUN AND RAIN

The main factors that affect climate and vegetation are temperature and humidity.

Climate in the various parts of the world is determined by how much sunlight an area receives and how much rain falls at different times of the year. Distance from the equator is a factor, also, as is position in relation to the prevailing winds that may or may not bring moisture from the oceans.

New York   London   Omsk   Singapore

Rainfall

Temperature

The colors in this diagram represent the many kinds of climates in the world. Although they look complex and interlinked, the same broad bands of vegetation are found both north and south of the equator.

Right:
The charts in this diagram compare typical rainfall amounts and climate temperatures throughout the world.

Rainfall

Temperature

CLIMATE ZONES

Manaus   Alice Springs   Lagos

TEMPERATE TAKEOVER

No open land will remain barren for long if it is possible for plants to grow. At the end of the last Ice Age, about 10,000 years ago, the land left by retreating glaciers was quickly colonized by vegetation.

First came small plants, such as mosses and lichens, which started to create soil. Then came tough grasses and heathers. The first trees were small, hardy types, such as birch and ash, followed by conifers. Then, as the climate improved, deciduous forest was established.

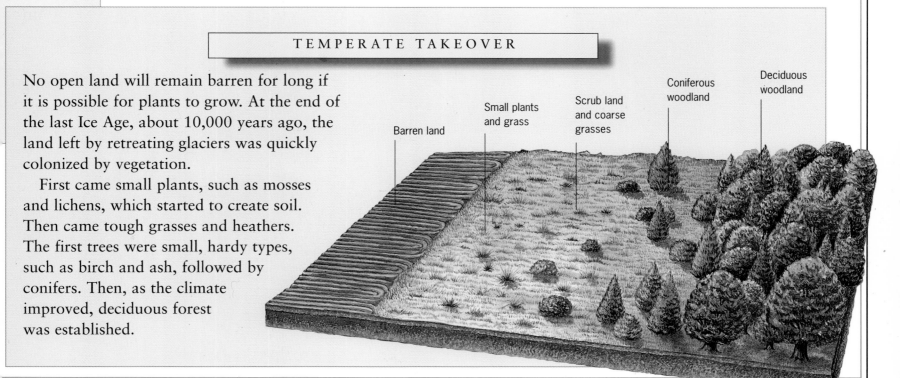

Barren land   Small plants and grass   Scrub land and coarse grasses   Coniferous woodland   Deciduous woodland

Ocean Currents

See also:
- **Rivers** p. 38
- **... and Deltas** p. 42
- **Seas and Tides** p. 60
- **Changing Coasts** p. 62

MORE THAN two-thirds of Earth's surface is covered with water, and this water is in constant motion. Surface currents are driven by winds, while deep currents are driven by the circulation of warm and cold water, and by the Coriolis effect. These powerful currents move water across entire oceans, bringing warm weather to cold coastal areas and cooling regions that would otherwise be hot.

ICEBERG CARRIERS
The ocean off the coast of Labrador has a cold southerly current that brings drifting icebergs, which have broken away from Greenland and the neighboring Labrador Coast, along with it. Over 700 icebergs move south on this current each year, some traveling many hundreds of miles.

MEDDIES
Every time the tide goes in and out of the Mediterranean, it surges through the Strait of Gibraltar. As the warm, salty seawater flows beneath the cooler, bouyant water of the Atlantic Ocean, it forms massive rotating currents known as "Meddies."

OCEAN PATTERNS
The ocean can provide many surprising images, as these pictures show. Different currents and depths of water can show up as distinct patterns, even on hand-held satellite images. These images help oceanographers plot the movements of these vast bodies of water.

PACIFIC SWIRL
This mass of swirling water in the Sea of Japan is many hundreds of miles (km) wide. It forms part of a gyre as the Kuroshia, Oyashio, and North Pacific currents meet.

OCEAN CORKSCREWS

The surface currents of the oceans are controlled by the global wind pattern. The main ocean current is called a gyre. Currents sweep around the ocean basins, moving clockwise in the Northern Hemisphere, and counter-clockwise in the Southern Hemisphere. The various "legs" of a gyre produce warm currents along the western sides of the oceans and cold currents along the eastern sides. In the North Atlantic, the western current, known as the Gulf Stream, brings warm water across the Atlantic from the West Indies to northern Europe.

SHIFTING SANDS

Ocean currents have a strong influence on the shape of the coastline. When currents move in one prevailing direction, they carry the sand along the shoreline in that direction, gradually building sand bars away from the land. When the current sweeps past a bay, the sand bar curves back, forming a hook with eddies swirling around the tip.

A sand bar is a constantly shifting piece of land. England's Spurn Point has rebuilt itself six or seven times over the course of the last 200 years.

Below:
Cape Cod in Massachusetts is a sandspit with a characteristic curve at the tip. It is one of many spits produced by the North Atlantic Drift.

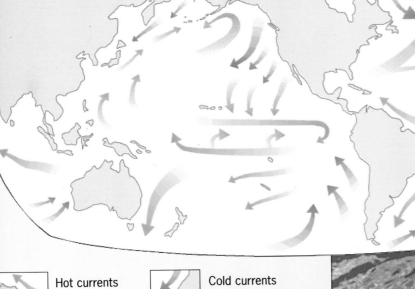

 Hot currents   Cold currents

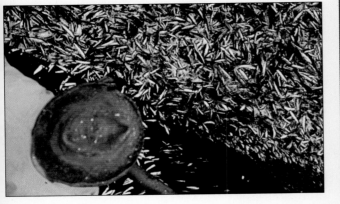

Above:
Cold, deep ocean currents, such as those in the North Atlantic and the Eastern Pacific, are rich in nutrients and support multitudes of fish.

El Niño

See also:
- **Ocean Currents** p. 56
- **Global Weather** p. 68
- **Clouds and Storms** p. 70

MARCH 17, 1997

FIRST WAVE
The progress of the 1997–98 El Niño was charted with false-color photographs taken by the U.S. National Oceanographic and Atmospheric Administration satellite.

MARCH 21, 1997

BUILD-UP
The first photograph on March 17 (above) shows the warm water (red and white) in the equatorial west Pacific. Four days later (right), the warm water was beginning to reach eastward.

THE NORTHEAST and southeast trade winds in the Pacific combine to drive warm surface waters westward. Every few years, however, these waters change direction and flow eastward. This change in the ocean circulation, because of a change in the winds, has an effect on climates all over the globe. The effect is known as El Niño, or "the child," because it often occurs around Christmastime.

MAKING WAVES

In the past, an El Niño effect has occurred once in ten years or so. The trade winds change direction from west to east, and warm surface waters accumulated in the west begin to move eastward, pooling in the eastern Pacific and beginning El Niño. The unaccustomed warm water in the eastern Pacific prevents the usual rise of cold water from the deep trenches of the ocean bed. In the 1990s, the El Niño effect has become so frequent and long-lasting it is almost the norm and will likely have an enduring influence on world climates.

Far Left:
Even as far away as Africa, El Niño has upset the balance of sun and rain.

EVENT HORIZON
A month later, the warm water had reached the coast of South America, bringing unseasonably warm conditions to the Galápagos Islands and to Peru, which suffered flooding and violent storms. It also destroyed the Peruvian anchovy harvest.

ALTERING CLIMATE

El Niño affects far more than just the eastern Pacific. Land areas in the western Pacific are prone to typhoons, like the one that killed 6,000 people in the Philippines in 1991. Australia, Africa, and Southeast Asia suffer droughts that cause poor harvests. The tinder-dry conditions have also contributed to disastrous fires in the rain forests of Sumatra and Borneo. These fires destroy wildlife and cause widespread pollution.

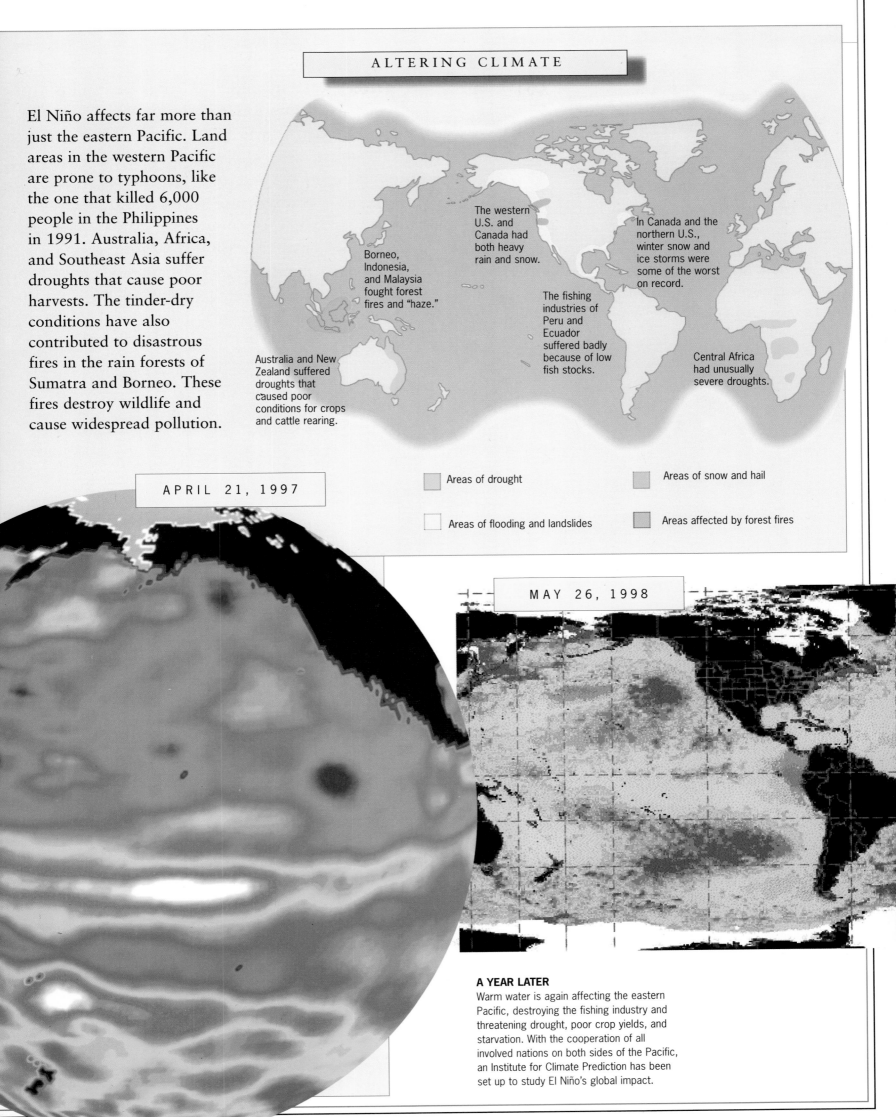

The western U.S. and Canada had both heavy rain and snow.

In Canada and the northern U.S., winter snow and ice storms were some of the worst on record.

Borneo, Indonesia, and Malaysia fought forest fires and "haze."

The fishing industries of Peru and Ecuador suffered badly because of low fish stocks.

Central Africa had unusually severe droughts.

Australia and New Zealand suffered droughts that caused poor conditions for crops and cattle rearing.

APRIL 21, 1997

Areas of drought

Areas of flooding and landslides

Areas of snow and hail

Areas affected by forest fires

MAY 26, 1998

A YEAR LATER

Warm water is again affecting the eastern Pacific, destroying the fishing industry and threatening drought, poor crop yields, and starvation. With the cooperation of all involved nations on both sides of the Pacific, an Institute for Climate Prediction has been set up to study El Niño's global impact.

Seas and Tides

See also:
- **Changing Coasts** *p. 62*
- **Global Weather** *p. 68*
- **Clouds and Storms** *p. 70*

DEEP BLUE HOLES

The ocean can be divided into depth zones. Closest to land, the continental shelf is only about 450 feet (137 m) at its deepest point, although the Tongue of the Ocean in the Bahamas (*below*) is over 1 mile (1.6 km) deep. Beyond this zone, the continental slope drops away to the abyssal plain, the true ocean floor, with an average depth of 12,000 feet (3,658 m). Some oceans have deep trenches. The deepest, over 36,000 feet (10,973 m) is the Mariana Trench in the western Pacific.

VISIT A seashore and you will see constant change. Twice a day, tides gradually creep up the beach, then slowly retreat again. Over a month (28 days), the tides alternate between strong spring tides and weaker neap tides, depending on the alignment of the Sun, the Moon, and Earth.

Wind blowing over the surface of the water piles the water up into ridges, creating waves that move in the direction of the wind. Big waves develop during storms and small ripples when winds are calm.

BREAKERS ON THE SHORE

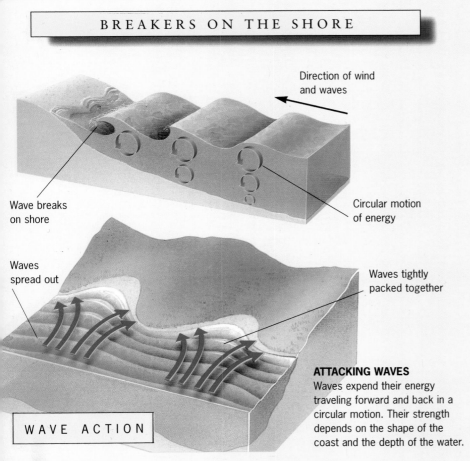

Direction of wind and waves

Circular motion of energy

Wave breaks on shore

Waves spread out

Waves tightly packed together

ATTACKING WAVES
Waves expend their energy traveling forward and back in a circular motion. Their strength depends on the shape of the coast and the depth of the water.

WAVE ACTION

Winds passing over the surface of the ocean whip it up into waves, blasting the water particles forward and back in a circular motion. When a wave reaches shallow water, the circular motion drags on the bottom, and the wave topples over, forming a breaker.

Although the water itself is moving only with limited action, wave disturbance can travel thousands of miles (km). As a wave approaches land, it tends to curve around any exposed headlands, attacking their cliffs from either side.

MOON POWER

As Earth and the Moon move around each other, bulges of water, or tides, are dragged toward the Moon on one side of Earth, and pulled away on the other. In the diagram below, the movement of the Moon is exaggerated, and the harbor is marked **X**.

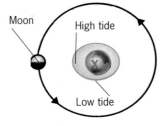

Moon

High tide

Low tide

SEPTEMBER 1
It is high tide at harbor X, because the Moon is directly overhead and is pulling the water toward it.

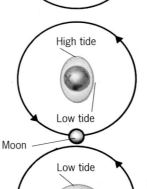

High tide

Low tide

Moon

SEPTEMBER 8
Harbor X is now at low tide, because the Moon has moved 90° around Earth.

Low tide

Moon

High tide

SEPTEMBER 15
Harbor X is at high tide again, because a bulge of water has been created by the movement of Earth around the Moon.

Moon

High tide

Low tide

SEPTEMBER 22
It is low tide again at harbor X, because, once more, it is halfway between the tidal bulges.

HIGH RISE AND FALL

The shape of the shoreline has an effect on tides. The highest tides occur where there are long bays and inlets, forcing the rising water into narrow gaps.

Canada's Bay of Fundy (*right*) has a tidal range of 44 feet (13 m) at the strong spring tides, when the Sun and Moon are exerting a pull together.

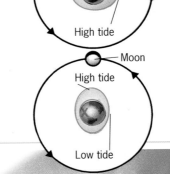

Changing Coasts

See also:
- **Eroding Earth** *p. 44*
- **Ocean Currents** *p. 56*
- **Seas and Tides** *p. 60*

Below:

A Landsat compositional mosaic of the British Isles shows many examples of changing coastal scenery. Since the end of the Ice Age, the region has gradually been tilting, with northern Scotland rising out of the water and southern England slowly becoming submerged.

RISING LAND
Around much of Scotland, the coastline has raised beaches – shelves of sand tens of feet (m) above present-day beaches, which represent the levels of the beaches during the Ice Age.

SCOTTISH FJORDS
On the west coast of Scotland, mountains that are 400 million years old are being attacked by the rough seas of the Atlantic, producing the typical eroded coastline of sea lochs and peninsulas.

THE BOUNDARY between land and sea is constantly changing. In some areas, the land is being pounded and slowly worn away by the action of the sea. Elsewhere, the sea is depositing sand and gravel or shingle along the shore, gradually building the coastline. The results are two types of coastlines. An eroded coast, such as the west coast of Scotland, is admired for its rugged grandeur. A coast with sand and stone provides vacationers with beautiful beaches.

HARD ROCKS, SOFT ROCKS

Mountain ranges jutting out into the sea are constantly broken down and eroded by the perpetual pounding of waves. Such a coastline is jagged, with many headlands and inlets.

The material broken away from the land on an eroded coast often ends up on another coast that is slowly being built up. The broken rocky material is slowly reduced to sand and gravel by the action of the sea. It is then spread by waves along beaches where the land is flatter. Looking down from the sky, a coastline that is gradually being built up has a smooth margin that is often swept into spits and sand bars by prevailing sea currents.

THE NORTH SEA
The North Sea rests on a low continental shelf. The shelf is crossed from north to south by shallow "stretch marks" that indicate a slowly expanding seabed.

SOUTHWESTERN BRITAIN
The estuaries of Devon and Cornwall are flooded river valleys, submerged over the last few thousand years.

FORCES AT WORK

Along a coast that is being built up rather than eroded, sand and gravel are constantly on the move. Waves strike the coast at an angle and wash the sand in a diagonal path up the beach. Some of the sand is washed right back down again in the backwash, for the next wave to wash up at an angle. In this way, a process known as beach drift, or longshore drift, sand and gravel form a zigzag path along the beach.

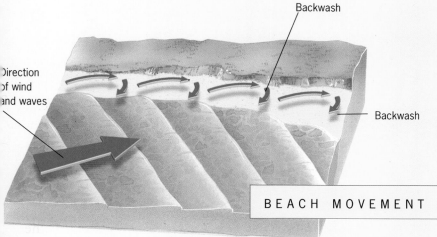

BEACH MOVEMENT

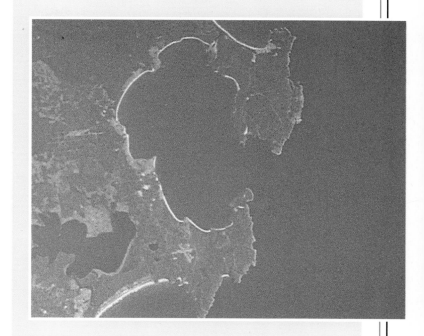

BAY OF WHALES

When beach drift meets an inlet, the deposits form a sand bar across the mouth, creating a shallow lagoon. If the sand bar is across a river mouth, it forms a half-bar, or spit.

When beach drift meets a headland, it builds a spit out into the sea. Sometimes the spit reaches as far out as an island, joining the island to the mainland. This kind of spit is called a tombolo. Jervis Bay in Australia is flanked by two tombolos.

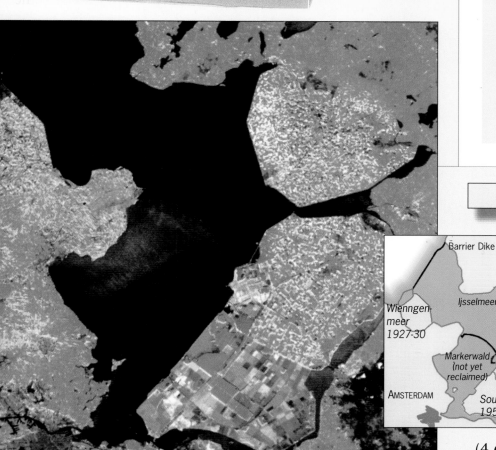

WINDMILLS AND WATER

Since the 7th century, the shallow inlets of the Netherlands have gradually been walled off into "polders" and pumped out to provide farm land – 3,000 square miles (7,770 sq km) in the past 800 years. Water in this low land, some of it 15 feet (4.6 m) below sea level, has to constantly be drained, using ditches, canals, pumps, and the traditional windmills.

Coral Islands

See also:
- **Volcano!** *p. 20*
- **Spreading Rifts** *p. 22*
- **Rivers** *p. 38*
- **. . . and Deltas** *p. 42*

RAIATEA
The single narrow fringing reef that surrounds both Raiatea and Tahaa can clearly be seen.

Below:
The Society Islands in French Polynesia display all types of coral growth. They stretch from the southeast to the northwest. The islands in the southeast (top left) are the youngest.

Corals are tiny organisms found in shallow tropical seas. Ranging in size from one-tenth of an inch (2.5 mm) to several inches (cm), they live in large colonies, in limestone shells. As each organism dies, a new one grows on top of its skeleton, constructing, over thousands of years, huge masses of limestone, called reefs. The Great Barrier Reef, along the northeastern coast of Australia, extends 1,250 miles (2,011 km).

Coral reefs provide a haven for all kinds of marine wildlife. Unfortunately, coral is very delicate, so it is vulnerable to the effects of tourism, commercial fishing, and environmental pollution.

BORA BORA
This classic island is hundreds of thousands of years older than its two sister islands *(left)*. It has a well-developed barrier reef on all sides, as well as broad reef flats.

TAHAA
This island has subsided slightly more than its sister Raiatea, and it has a barrier reef off shore. Both islands have high volcanic valleys with steeply eroded and wooded sides that end in a thin strip of beach.

THE LIFE AND DEATH OF A CORAL ISLAND

When an island is formed by volcanic action, coral builds up around the coast, forming a fringing reef. Later, the island may sink and become smaller as the seafloor subsides. As the reef continues to grow, it is separated from the sinking island by a lagoon, forming a barrier reef. When the island sinks completely, only the coral is left, forming a ring-shaped reef called an atoll.

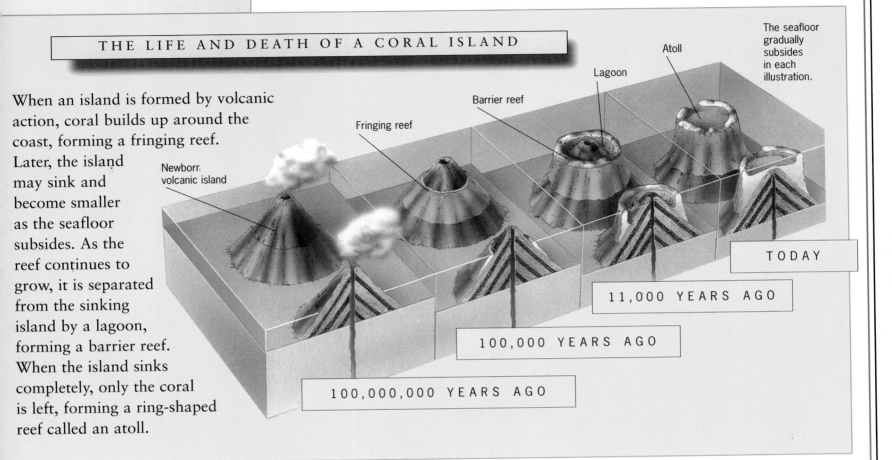

The seafloor gradually subsides in each illustration.

Newborn volcanic island

Fringing reef

Barrier reef

Lagoon

Atoll

TODAY

11,000 YEARS AGO

100,000 YEARS AGO

100,000,000 YEARS AGO

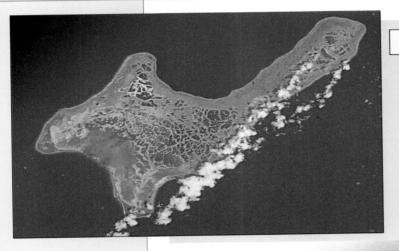

THE WORLD'S BIGGEST ATOLL

Kiritimati, previously known as Christmas Island, is the largest atoll in the Pacific Ocean. It was discovered on Christmas Eve, in 1777, by Captain Cook. Because of its remote position and its barrenness, it was used as a testing site for nuclear weapons in the 1950s and 1960s.

TUPAI
This island is the oldest of the Society Islands shown. The central island has completely subsided, leaving a series of submerged reefs and lagoons, called an atoll. There are only three gaps in the reef.

Right:
In this view of a typical Pacific coral island, the sea is shallow and exceptionally clear. A reef is growing only a few inches (cm) below the surface of the water.

Unseen Forces

*Under the sea, on land,
and in the air, hidden forces
are slowly altering the balance
of our living planet.*

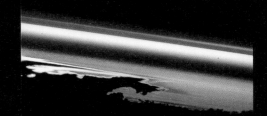

Global Weather

See also:
- **The Air Around Us** *p. 14*
- **Ocean Currents** *p. 56*
- **El Niño** *p. 58*
- **Clouds and Storms** *p. 70*

FAST LANES IN THE SKY

High in the atmosphere is a mysterious system of very fast winds, called jet streams. They are tubelike cores of high-speed winds that encircle Earth. A jet stream is 100 miles (161 km) wide and 2 to 5 miles (3 to 8 km) deep. The winds blow eastward at speeds of up to 250 mph (402 kmph). Eastbound airliners use jet streams to save time and fuel.

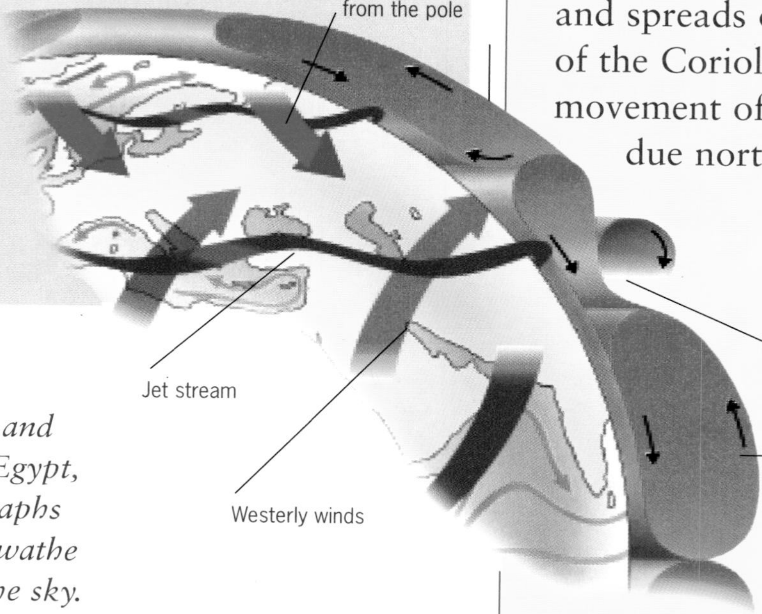

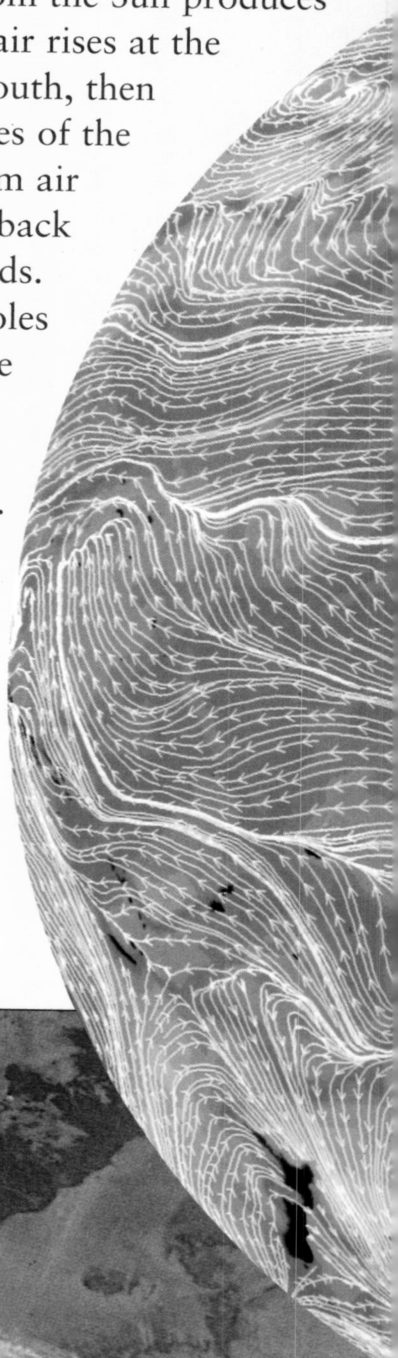

Below:
Over the Red Sea and the Nile River in Egypt, a satellite photographs a jet stream as a swathe of clouds across the sky.

Cold air from the pole

Jet stream

Westerly winds

Cold air descending

Trade winds

Hot air rising

OUR WEATHER is the result of wind movement across Earth. Energy from the Sun produces the heat at the equator. Hot air rises at the equator, spreads north and south, then descends at about the latitudes of the Tropics. From there, the warm air spreads out to the poles and back to the equator as surface winds. Cold air descends over the poles and spreads outward. Because of the Coriolis effect, the movement of winds is not due north and due south.

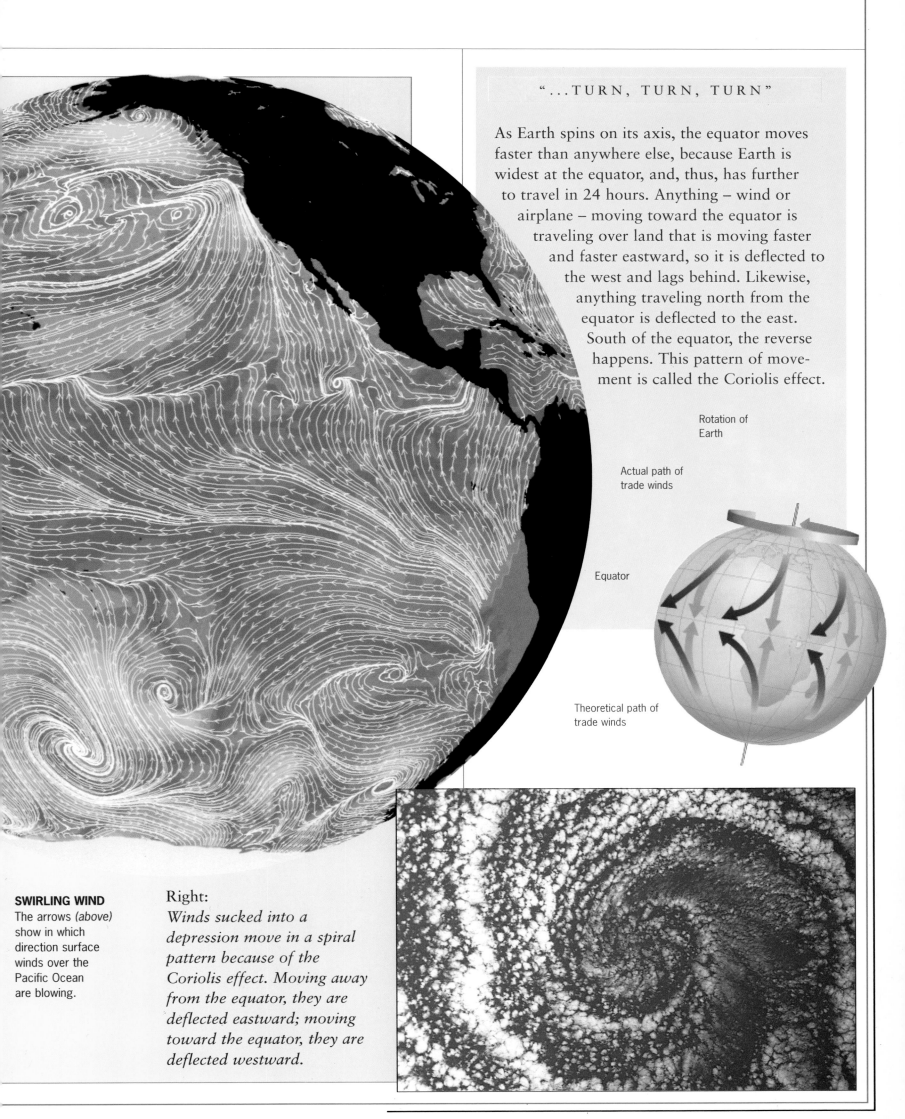

"...TURN, TURN, TURN"

As Earth spins on its axis, the equator moves faster than anywhere else, because Earth is widest at the equator, and, thus, has further to travel in 24 hours. Anything – wind or airplane – moving toward the equator is traveling over land that is moving faster and faster eastward, so it is deflected to the west and lags behind. Likewise, anything traveling north from the equator is deflected to the east. South of the equator, the reverse happens. This pattern of movement is called the Coriolis effect.

Rotation of Earth

Actual path of trade winds

Equator

Theoretical path of trade winds

SWIRLING WIND
The arrows (above) show in which direction surface winds over the Pacific Ocean are blowing.

Right:
Winds sucked into a depression move in a spiral pattern because of the Coriolis effect. Moving away from the equator, they are deflected eastward; moving toward the equator, they are deflected westward.

Clouds and Storms

See also:
- **The Air Around Us** *p. 14*
- **Ocean Currents** *p. 56*
- **El Niño** *p. 58*
- **Killer Winds** *p. 72*

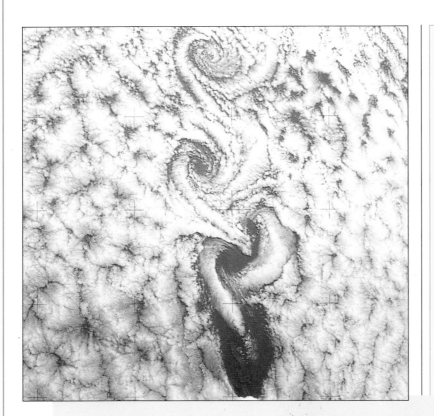

WATER, WHICH is essential for life on Earth, exists in three forms. Depending on temperature and air pressure, water can exist as a liquid, as a solid (ice), or as a gas (vapor).

Clouds form when water vapor in the air condenses into tiny droplets of water. In warm clouds, swirling air currents make the droplets collide and join together into larger droplets, which eventually fall as rain. Warm clouds are the white, fluffy cumulus clouds or the low, gray stratus clouds.

If a cloud has a temperature below freezing, the water vapor turns into ice crystals. These are the high cirrus clouds. They look more feathery and wispy than fluffy cumulus clouds.

THE PATTERNS IN THE SKY SHOW

Above and below: *Cloud patterns formed by wind show how, like water, wind flows around an obstruction. In Western Australia, clouds have formed over peaks of the Chichester range. These "pointed" clouds are rare.*

We are all familiar with the appearance of clouds as seen from below – the dark underbelly of storm clouds or the high, wispy mare's tails that suggest a change of weather is on the way. Clouds look even more spectacular from above, with their shapes depending on whether there is land or sea beneath them.

Left: *When wind blows over a flat hillcrest, wavelike wind currents can build up clouds downwind, to the left of the obstacle. These cloud waves were photographed over South Australia.*

THE SOUND AND LIGHT SHOW

Thunderclouds form in warm, moist, rapidly rising air. As the air rises, the moisture condenses, forming towering cumulonimbus clouds. Air circulation is so strong in these clouds that the raindrops cannot fall. They just become bigger and more unstable. Eventually, they break apart, releasing an electric charge. The electricity discharged to the ground forms a lightning flash, and the air expands with a crack of thunder.

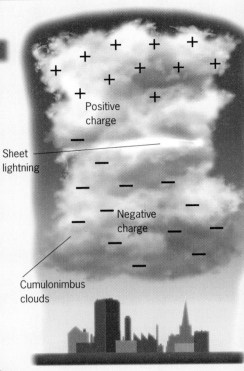

Positive charge

Sheet lightning

Negative charge

Cumulonimbus clouds

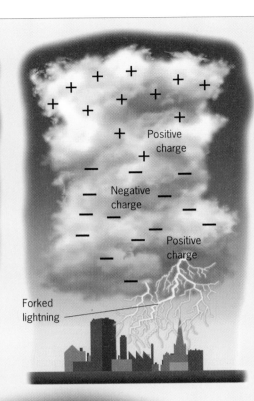

Positive charge

Negative charge

Positive charge

Forked lightning

Above and right:
A tropical storm over Brazil shows off its icy "anvil" thunderhead, while forked lightning hits the desert.

Killer Winds

See also:
- **The Air Around Us** *p. 14*
- **Ocean Currents** *p. 56*
- **Global Weather** *p. 68*
- **Clouds and Storms** *p. 70*

AUGUST 25, 1992
"ANDREW" APPROACHES LOUISIANA

Above and right:
In August 1992, hurricane Andrew caused the most damage and highest death toll of any hurricane in living memory. Between August 23 and August 27, it was responsible for 52 deaths and $22 billion of damage (below) *in the Bahamas, Louisiana, and Florida.*

AUGUST 26, 1992
"ANDREW" HITS
THE COAST

THE TWO most powerful storms known to man are hurricanes and tornados. Both can wreak havoc on an almost unimaginable scale, within seconds and with little warning.

THE COILED SERPENT

Hurricanes develop in hot climates, when areas of low atmospheric pressure form over tropical oceans. Large amounts of moisture evaporate, and, as the hot air rises, more air is drawn in at sea level with great force. The wind spirals inward and upward, counterclockwise around a central "eye," producing the hurricane.

The Coriolis effect, produced by the difference in the rotation speed of Earth close to and away from the equator, is responsible for the spiral structure and the westward movement of the storm system.

HOW HURRICANES FORM

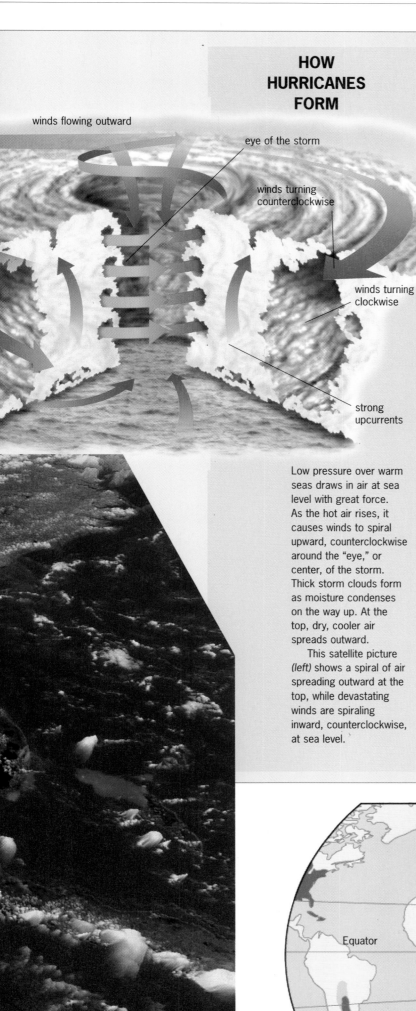

winds flowing outward

eye of the storm

winds turning counterclockwise

winds turning clockwise

strong upcurrents

Low pressure over warm seas draws in air at sea level with great force. As the hot air rises, it causes winds to spiral upward, counterclockwise around the "eye," or center, of the storm. Thick storm clouds form as moisture condenses on the way up. At the top, dry, cooler air spreads outward.

This satellite picture *(left)* shows a spiral of air spreading outward at the top, while devastating winds are spiraling inward, counterclockwise, at sea level.

"LET'S TWIST AGAIN..."

Tornados develop when hot, moist and cold, dry air masses meet and shear past each other during a thunderstorm. This causes small areas of intense low pressure that bring air swirling inward, counterclockwise, in a narrow column to form the tornado. The funnel-shaped cloud quickly extends to the ground and swirls across land at speeds of more than 100 mph (161 kmph). It destroys buildings, sucks up people and vehicles, and flattens everything in its path.

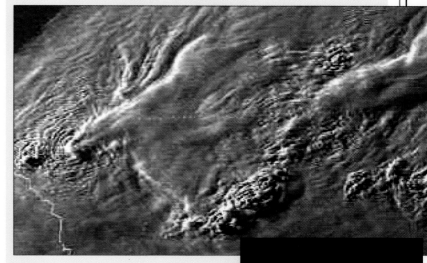

Above and right:
Tornados seen over Texas – from a weather satellite and from the ground.

WHERE THE WINDS CAN KILL
The map below shows areas, worldwide, that are affected by severe storms, such as hurricanes and tornadoes. Areas of the most intense storms are shown in red, and areas where these storms are less likely are shaded pink.

Tropic of Cancer

Equator

Tropic of Capricorn

Marks of Man

See also:
- **Squashed Forests** *p. 32*
- **Black Gold** *p. 34*
- **Shifting Deserts** *p. 46*
- **Moving Bands** *p. 54*

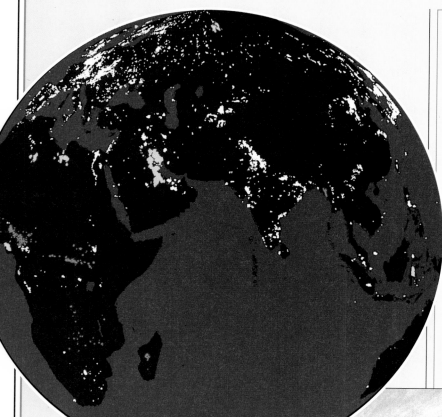

HUMANS HAVE left their marks on many parts of Earth's surface – some of them for good reasons, others misguided. Whatever the causes, the effects are plain to see, and from space, they are even more evident.

The Great Wall of China can easily be recognized from an orbiting spacecraft. Tracks can be traced in the desert and ruined cities plotted in rain forest mountains. The remote sensing equipment on satellites can shed light on an ancient past as easily as observing the progress of a modern war.

At night, our planet shimmers with light, like fireflies hovering in the sky on a warm summer evening.

Above:
This computer-enhanced view of Earth without cloud cover shows the intensity of lights from cities in Europe, the Middle East, and the Indian subcontinent compared with that from the sparsely developed continent of Africa.

Right:
In the middle of Siberian Russia, Omsk is a city built alongside the tracks of the Trans-Siberian Railway. Drifting snow and a low camera angle accentuate the gridlike pattern of this city in the "middle of nowhere."

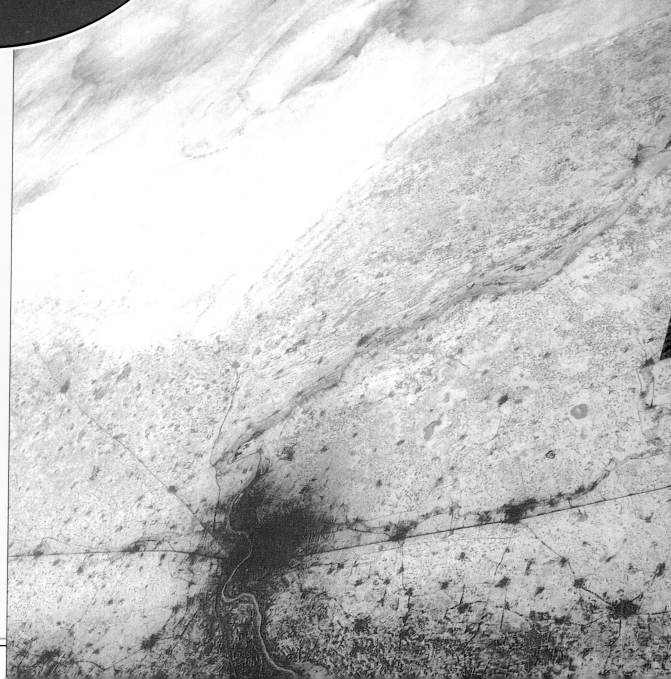

NATURAL AND MANMADE BOUNDARIES

The boundaries between different nations often can be better appreciated from space than from the ground, especially where there are political as well as natural boundaries. Political boundaries frequently lie along geographical features, such as rivers.

The Itaipú Dam Project is a joint Brazilian-Argentine hydroelectric power plant – the largest in the world. The main dam is 6 miles (10 km) long and 200 feet (61 m) high. Its output is about 12,600 megawatts.

Parana River

The boundary between Brazil (at right) and Argentina is marked by farm fields on the Brazilian side and managed forest between the Argentinian border and the river.

Iguassu Falls

The Iguassu River forms a natural boundary with the Parana River that encompasses two sides of a national park. Along this boundary lies the spectacular *Carartas del Iguassu*, or Iguassu Falls, which plunges 270 feet (82 m) into a steep canyon.

THE BRAZIL-ARGENTINA BORDER

Smoke from burning oil installations

WAR FROM THE AIR

Imaging from a remote sensor can track a tank in a desert or a platoon on a tundra. Similarly, a plume of oil smoke was tracked as soon as Saddam Hussein had ignited the oil wells *(opposite)* in his retreat from Kuwait in 1991. Scientists could analyze the clouds, determine their chemical makeup, and warn of potential problems.

Kuwait City

Holes in the Sky

See also:
- **The Air Around Us** *p. 14*
- **El Niño** *p. 58*
- **Global Weather** *p. 68*
- **Clouds and Storms** *p. 70*

A THINNING SHIELD

There is a layer in the atmosphere, 12 to 13 miles (19 to 21 km) above Earth, that is rich in a kind of oxygen called ozone. This ozone layer is important because it filters out ultraviolet (UV) radiation from the Sun.

Since the mid-1980s, scientists have recognized an annual thinning of the ozone layer, particularly over the poles. The most obvious cause seems to be chemical pollution, particularly chlorofluorocarbons (CFCs). Sunlight breaks down CFCs in the atmosphere, and released chlorine reduces the filtering properties of the ozone. The increase in UV radiation that reaches us can lead to skin cancers.

EARTH'S CLIMATE is constantly changing. We need to look only at the strata of ancient rocks or the ice layers in Greenland to see it. Although gases from volcanoes and hot springs have continually been altering the composition of the atmosphere, a mass of evidence suggests that climate is now changing much faster than normal – and we are the agents of this change. Industry and technology fill the atmosphere with pollutants, and chemical wastes modify its physics and chemistry. These changes are bound to affect our lives.

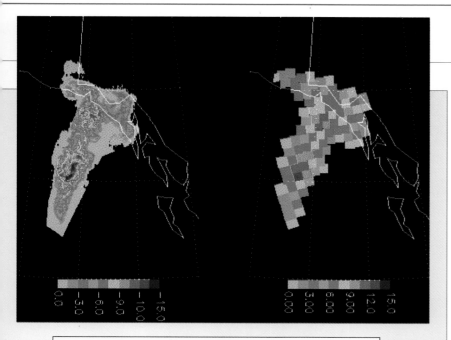

NO SMOKE WITHOUT FIRE

Erupting volcanoes, such as Mount Pinatubo and Mount St. Helens, belch out immense quantities of gas, dust, and ash into the atmosphere. Vehicles, power plants, and factories further pollute the atmosphere by releasing sulfur dioxide and nitrogen oxide. These pollutants can be carried great distances by winds and are removed only by rain or snow. Some of the chemicals released dissolve in rainwater, forming "acid rain," which has affected Earth by rotting crops, poisoning lakes, killing trees, and causing respiratory diseases.

THAT SINKING FEELING

Over the last 200 years or so, there has been a change in the atmosphere. By burning fossil fuels, industry has generated an increase of carbon dioxide. Other increased gases include methane and water vapor. All of these gases together produce the "greenhouse effect," which allows the Sun's rays to reach Earth's surface, but traps the heat radiated from the surface, increasing its temperature. On a world-wide scale this effect might produce global warming, which, among other consequences, could melt ice caps and raise sea level. Low-lying areas, such as Florida (*left*), would become very vulnerable.

AN EL NIÑO SIDESHOW

Early 1998 saw devastating fires in Borneo for the second year running, the result of "slash and burn" agriculture, in which areas of natural forest are burned to provide farmland. A simultaneous drought, as a result of the "El Niño effect," helped the fires rage out of control. Satellite sensors, over three month's time, showed the rise and fall of atmospheric haze in Southeast Asia, which caused severe health problems.

FEBRUARY 2, 1998

MARCH 21, 1998

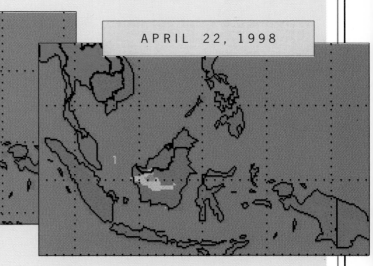

APRIL 22, 1998

Left:
The hole in the ozone layer was first detected by the British Antarctic Survey at Halley Bay in Antarctica in 1982. This first image was taken in 1988 by NASA's satellite TOMS. Since then, the hole has been getting larger.

Soiled Waters

See also:
- **The Air Around Us** p. 14
- **El Niño** p. 58
- **Global Weather** p. 68
- **Clouds and Storms** p. 70

Below:
Madagascar is running out of soil. It is being washed into the sea. The red stain in the water can be seen clearly in this shot, from the Space Shuttle, of the Betsiboka River outfall, with the Mozambique Channel at the top.

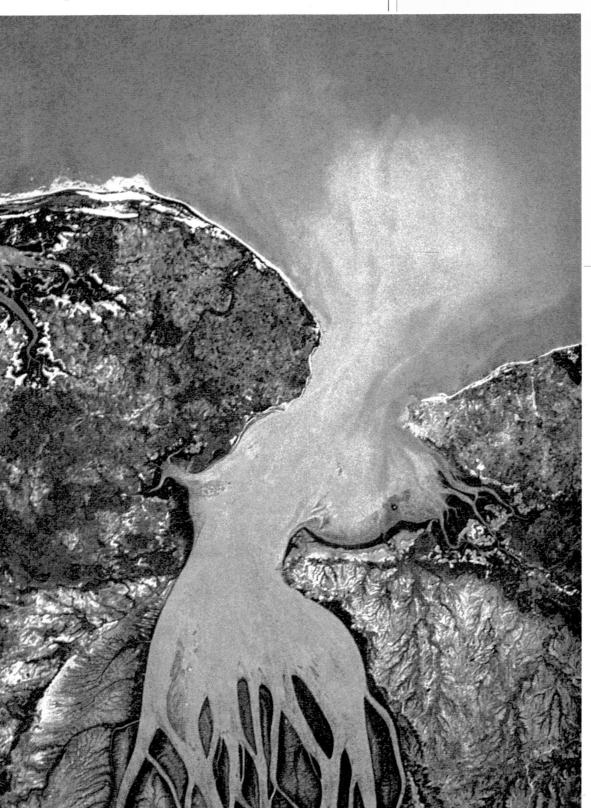

THE OCEAN has always been regarded as having an infinite capacity – a trash receptacle that could hold anything, regardless of what or how much was dumped into it. Sadly, this theory has proven untrue.

The enormous volume of human garbage and industrial waste built up over the centuries is now altering the composition and quality of the sea. This problem is most obvious in confined seas with poor circulation, such as the Mediterranean, and in areas bordering on busy ports and large cities. Recently, however, fears also have been expressed about even the deepest parts of the ocean floor.

A SPILL TOO MANY

Much of the world's economy is based on oil, which has to be transported by tanker from place to place. During the Arab-Israeli War in the 1960s, a new generation of "supertankers" was built to enable oil traffic to bypass the Suez Canal. The first big accident involving an oil supertanker was the oil spill from the *Torrey Canyon* off Cornwall, England, in 1967.

Opposite:
On March 24, 1989, the tanker Exxon Valdez *ran aground in Alaska, rupturing its tanks and spilling its load of crude oil. The resulting oil slick polluted the shoreline. The cleanup took years and cost millions.*

Below:
The Strait of Hormuz, at the bottom of the Persian Gulf, sees 20 percent of the world's oil traffic pass through its waters. Oil slicks, debris, and waste discharges are all killing its marine environment.

Top:
Tanker spills are spectacular, but most pollution comes from the discharge of machine wastes. Wildlife suffers just the same.

BUSY CROSSROADS

The nature of sea traffic means that some areas are much busier than others. The English Channel, the Cape of Good Hope, the Malay Straits, and the Strait of Hormuz are some of the busier waterways in the world, and are, therefore, the most vulnerable. International agencies, such as the Intergovernmental Maritime Consultative Organization, have been set up to minimize human impact on these areas by regulating sea traffic and advising on tanker design.

PART FOUR

Snapshots of Our World

*Fly by Earth –
four global views show us how
our planet looks from space.*

The Americas and the Eastern Pacific

THE TOPOGRAPHY of the Americas is one of the most varied to be found on our planet. The northern parts of Canada lie in the Arctic, while the southern tip of South America was, until recently (in geological time), joined to Antarctica.

North and Central America

North America occupies the northern part of the western hemisphere. It has a core of ancient rock, known as the Canadian Shield, that is rich in minerals and oil.

Huge mountain chains run down the eastern and western flanks of North America. The oldest mountains, formed some 400 million years ago, are the Appalachians in the east. They have been worn away by wind and rain for so long that they are now much lower than the younger, sharp-crested Rocky Mountains to the west.

Between these mountains lie the Great Plains – originally home to over 500 tribes of Native Americans, who were gradually ousted by immigrant white settlers.

Central America, the thin ribbon of land that joins the North and South American continents, includes over 30 countries and many small islands with mountainous, volcanic landscapes.

South America

The world's fourth largest continent straddles the equator and includes one of Earth's richest resources – the Amazon rain forest. This mass of virgin forest is a major source of the world's oxygen and contains almost half of all the world's living species. The Amazon River contains over one-fifth of the world's freshwater.

The Andes Mountains run down the western seaboard of South America.

Death Valley (left), in California (USA), is the lowest place on the American continents. Although the elevations there rise to over 10,000 feet (3,048 m), Death Valley is more famous for its lowest point at Badwater Basin – 282 feet (86 m) below sea level.

Lake Superior (below) is the largest of the Great Lakes and the second largest lake in the world. The Great Lakes were formed at the end of the Ice Age, when melting ice filled ground-out hollows.

The Amazon River (below), at 4,080 miles (6,565 km), is the world's second longest river and is surrounded by some of the most dense and most threatened equatorial rain forest in the world.

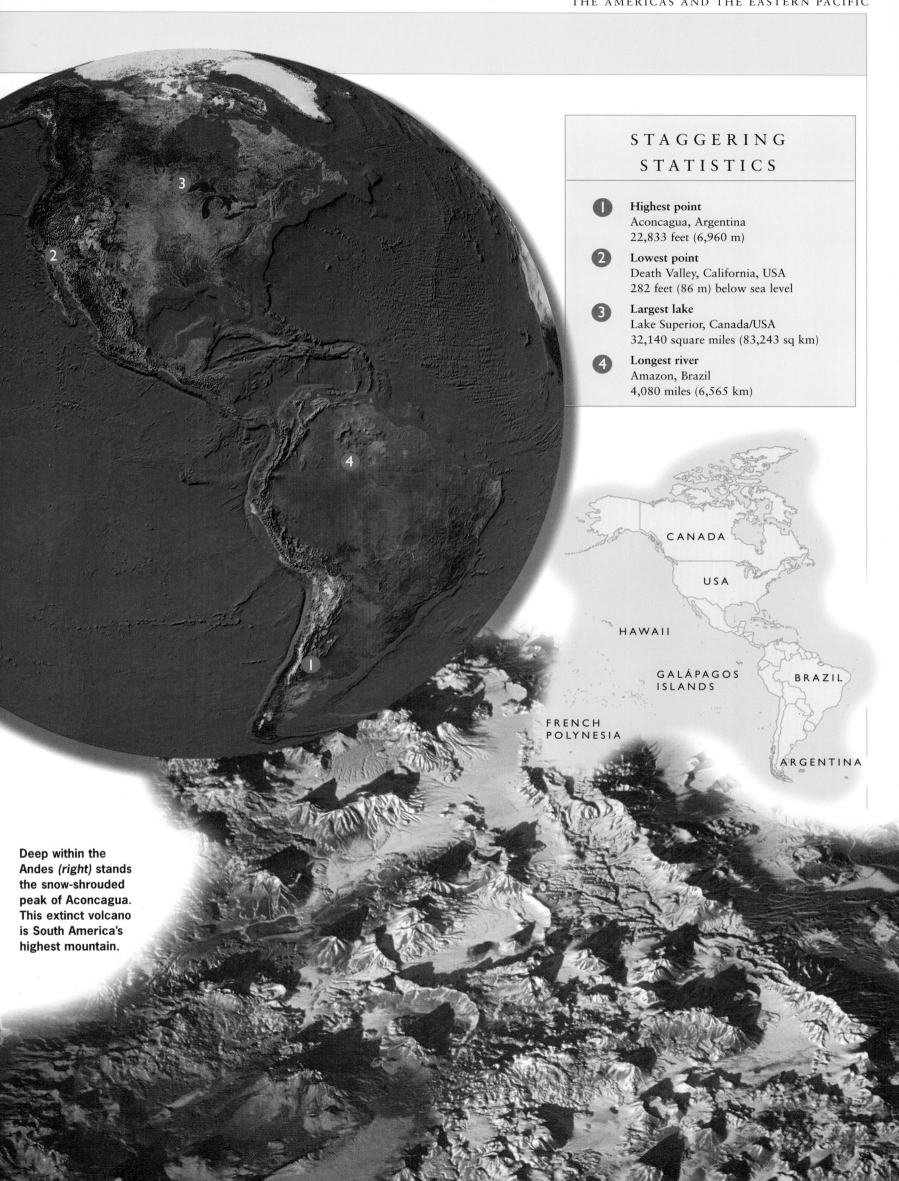

STAGGERING
STATISTICS

1 **Highest point**
Aconcagua, Argentina
22,833 feet (6,960 m)

2 **Lowest point**
Death Valley, California, USA
282 feet (86 m) below sea level

3 **Largest lake**
Lake Superior, Canada/USA
32,140 square miles (83,243 sq km)

4 **Longest river**
Amazon, Brazil
4,080 miles (6,565 km)

CANADA

USA

HAWAII

GALÁPAGOS
ISLANDS

BRAZIL

FRENCH
POLYNESIA

ARGENTINA

**Deep within the
Andes** *(right)* **stands
the snow-shrouded
peak of Aconcagua.
This extinct volcano
is South America's
highest mountain.**

Europe and Africa

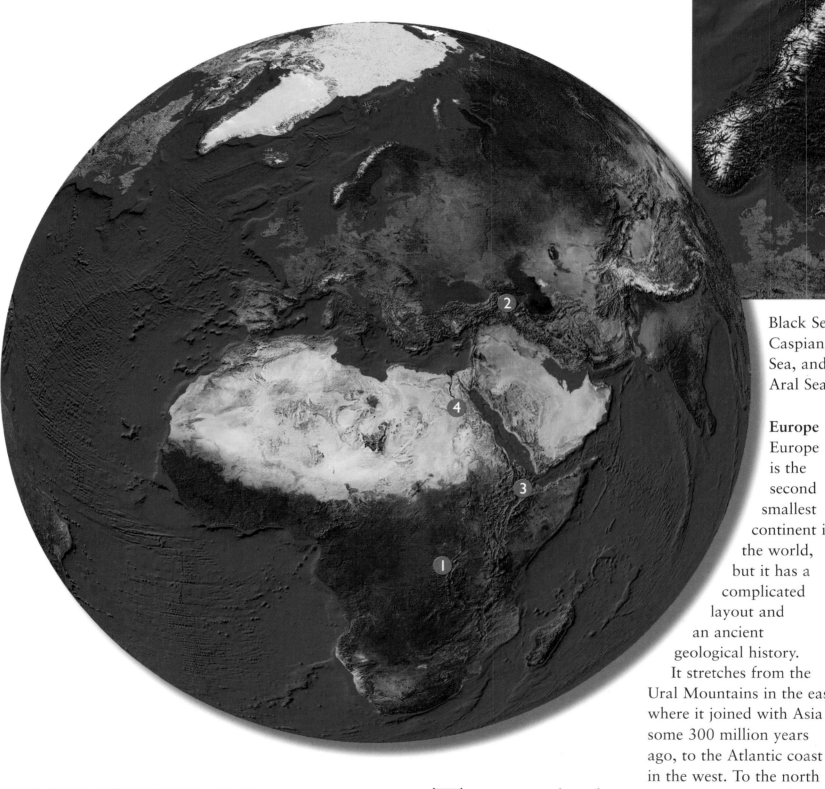

Black Sea,
Caspian
Sea, and
Aral Sea.

Europe
Europe
is the
second
smallest
continent in
the world,
but it has a
complicated
layout and
an ancient
geological history.
It stretches from the
Ural Mountains in the east,
where it joined with Asia
some 300 million years
ago, to the Atlantic coast
in the west. To the north
are the mountains of
Scotland and Norway,
which are approximately
400 million years old.
To the south are fold
mountains – the Atlas
Mountains in northern
Africa, the Apennines, the
Alps, and the Carpathians
– that are still forming as
Europe and Africa slowly
slide past one another.

THE NORTH and south
continental landmasses
were once separated by the
mighty Tethys Ocean.
That ocean has almost
disappeared as Africa has
slowly moved northeast
toward Europe, folding
and compacting the
mountains in between,
leaving only the "puddles"
of the Mediterranean,

STAGGERING STATISTICS

1 **Highest point in Africa**
Kilimanjaro, Tanzania 19,364 feet (5,902 m)

2 **Highest point in Europe**
Mount Elbrus, Russia 18,517 feet (5,644 m)

3 **Lowest point**
Lac Assal, Djibouti 471 feet (144 m) below sea level

4 **Longest river (in the world)**
Nile, Egypt 4,160 miles (6,693 km)

The northernmost part of Europe *(left)* lies inside the Arctic Circle, where the conifer forests of Norway, Sweden, and Finland give way to icy plains. All of Scandinavia was covered with glaciers during the last Ice Age, and the land, relieved of the great weight of ice, is still rising.

The movement of Africa is slowly stretching Europe in an east-west direction, producing the rift valleys of the Rhône and the Rhine, and the North Sea oil fields. The complex arrangement of bays, lochs, peninsulas, fjords, and inlets gives Europe the longest coastline of any continent.

Europe's climate is also complex, ranging from the balmy Mediterranean in the south, to areas in the north where the warm westerlies meet the cold polar easterlies, creating unstable weather conditions. Eastern Europe, far from the sea, has a continental climate, with very hot summers and very cold winters.

Africa

Africa is about three times the size of Europe and is built around chunks of ancient metamorphic rock. A system of rift valleys runs up the eastern side of the continent, marking a line where the continent will,

one day, tear itself apart. Madagascar has already broken away, and East Africa might also become an island. The Great Rift Valley system, formed over some five million years, continues up East Africa into Ethiopia and the Red Sea. Based on recent discoveries, this Rift Valley is where mankind first evolved two million or more years ago, then spread out to colonize the world.

The west coast of Africa reflects the east coast of South America, to which it was once joined.

Africa is crossed by the equator, a region marked by tropical rain forest with tropical grasslands, called savannas, on either side. Beyond, are belts of desert – the Sahara in the north and the Kalahari in the south. The extreme north and south have a Mediterranean climate.

This false-color Landsat image *(below)* shows the Nile River with its delta, as well as the Sinai peninsula and the Red Sea. The Red Sea is slowly widening as part of the Rift Valley system. In time, it will link up with the Mediterranean, but not for many millions of years.

Asia, Australia, and the Western Pacific

THESE THREE vast areas, which include two continents, cover half the globe.

Asia

Asia is the largest continent in the world, accounting for about one-third of the total land surface of Earth. The islands of the East Indies stretch below the equator, while the northern tip of Siberia falls within the Arctic Circle.

In the west, Asia has been joined to Europe along the Ural Mountains for some 300 million years. In the east, it narrows to a point at the Bering Strait only 53 miles (85 km) from North America.

In the south, Asia is almost joined to Africa, but the Red Sea is gradually widening, pushing the two continents apart.

The highest mountains in the world – the Himalayas – were formed a mere 50 million years ago, when the Indian plate moved northward and collided with the Asian plate, forcing the younger rocks upward. That movement is still taking place. Plate movement also crumpled up rocks to form the islands of the East Indies.

Along the eastern coast of Asia, the Pacific Ocean floor is slowly being drawn down under the continent, resulting in the islands of Japan, the Philippines, the Kuriles, and the Aleutians.

The Tibetan plateau behind the Himalayas *(above)* is a windswept place. What agriculture is attempted there takes place in river valleys, such as the Yarlung Zangbo Jiang, where winter wheat and barley are grown.

Australia

Australia is the largest island continent in the world. It was once joined to Antarctica but broke off some 60 million years ago and drifted northward. It is still moving north and, eventually, will collide with Asia.

Australia lies across the Tropic of Capricorn, hence its interior desert and tropical grasslands. In the north, Australia has equatorial rain forest; in the south, it has a Mediterranean climate.

Eastern Australia has a chain of mountains, known as the Great Dividing Range, running north to south. Most of the population lives in the coastal strip between these mountains and the sea. One other notable range – the Olgas – lies in the center of Australia and includes the landmark Ayers Rock.

STAGGERING STATISTICS

1. **Highest point**
Mount Everest, Tibet 29,116 feet (8,875 m)

2. **Lowest point**
Dead Sea, Israel 1,293 feet (394 m) below sea level

3. **Largest lake, also the deepest in the world**
(5,710 feet/1,740 m) and the oldest (50 million years)
Baikal, Siberia 12,150 square miles (31,469 sq km)

4. **Longest river**
Lena, Russia 2,730 miles (4,393 km). Empties into the Arctic in a delta 240 miles (386 km) wide

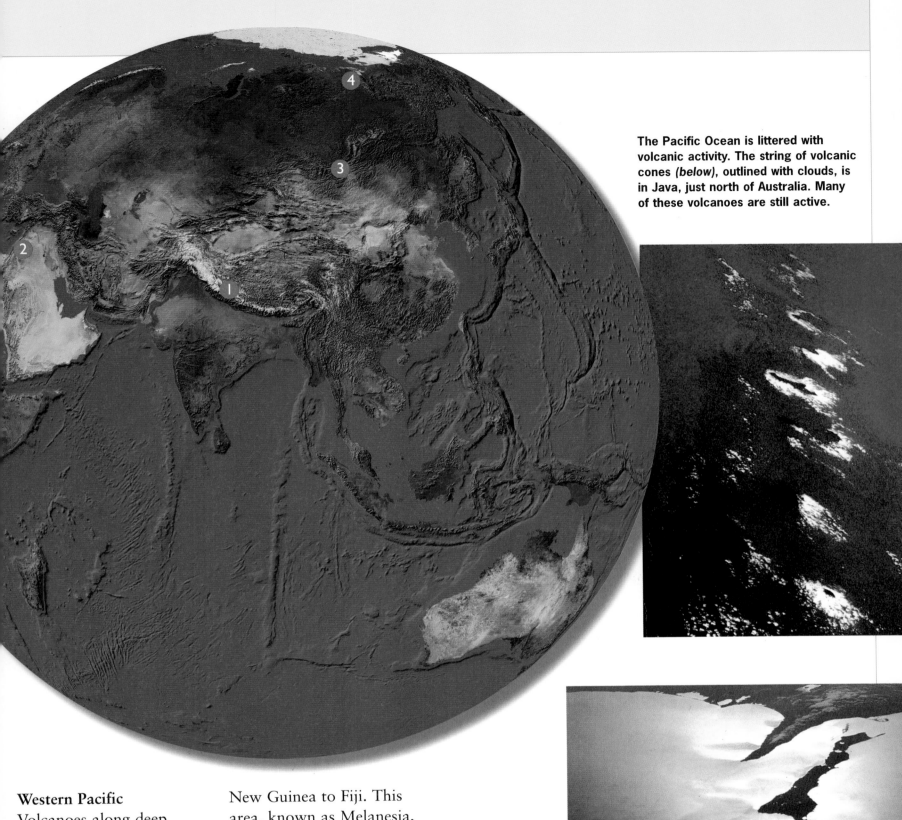

The Pacific Ocean is littered with volcanic activity. The string of volcanic cones *(below)*, outlined with clouds, is in Java, just north of Australia. Many of these volcanoes are still active.

Western Pacific

Volcanoes along deep trenches in the Western Pacific ocean have formed island arcs that include the Aleutian Islands, Japan, the Philippines, and New Guinea. Many of these volcanoes are still active and form the famous "Ring of Fire."

Another series of volcanic island chains, the remains of hotspot volcanoes, runs from New Guinea to Fiji. This area, known as Melanesia, was first colonized some 30,000 years ago by the same aborigine hunters from Southeast Asia who first colonized Australia.

The Kurile Islands *(right)* between Russia and Japan form part of the "Ring of Fire." Just west of these islands, the seafloor plunges to the greatest depths on Earth.

The North and South Poles

THE POLAR regions are the coldest places on Earth. At times, some areas within the Arctic and Antarctic Circles get no sunlight at all, and in some other areas, in summer, the Sun never sets. The poles themselves have six months of darkness followed by six months of daylight.

The North Pole

The North Pole lies in the Arctic Ocean. Its ice cap floats in the ocean with pack ice and only a few scattered islands lying beneath it. The only landmass of any size is Greenland, which also has an ice cap. Glaciers along the coast produce thousands of icebergs every year. These icebergs travel south to Newfoundland in the Labrador Current. Eventually, they are melted by the Gulf Stream.

The North Pole, although it is so far away from industrialized nations, suffers from pollution. DDT has been found in cod in the Barents Sea, and Caesium 137 from Chernobyl was found in northern Scandinavia.

The South Pole

At the South Pole, lies the continent of Antarctica. Twice the size of Australia, it is a typical continent with an old landmass at the center and mountain ranges along the edges. Most of the landmass is covered with ice, the

weight of which is so great that it presses down the interior below sea level. Consisting mainly of mountains that protrude through the ice, only about one percent of the Antarctic is free from ice. These few parts of the coastal plain are cold and barren, but the summer sunlight produces blooms of algae in the sea that attract multitudes of fish. The fish, in turn, are hunted by seals and flocks of penguins.

There are active volcanoes in the Antarctic, including Mount Erebus, the most southerly active volcano in the world.

Greenland (left) is almost totally covered by an ice cap. If the ice melted, the land on which it rested would rise by about 3 feet (1 m).

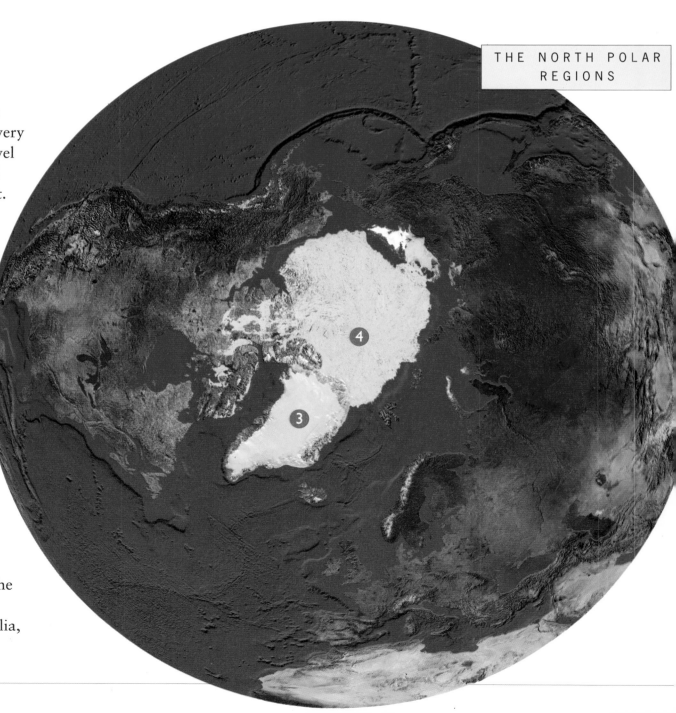

THE NORTH POLAR REGIONS

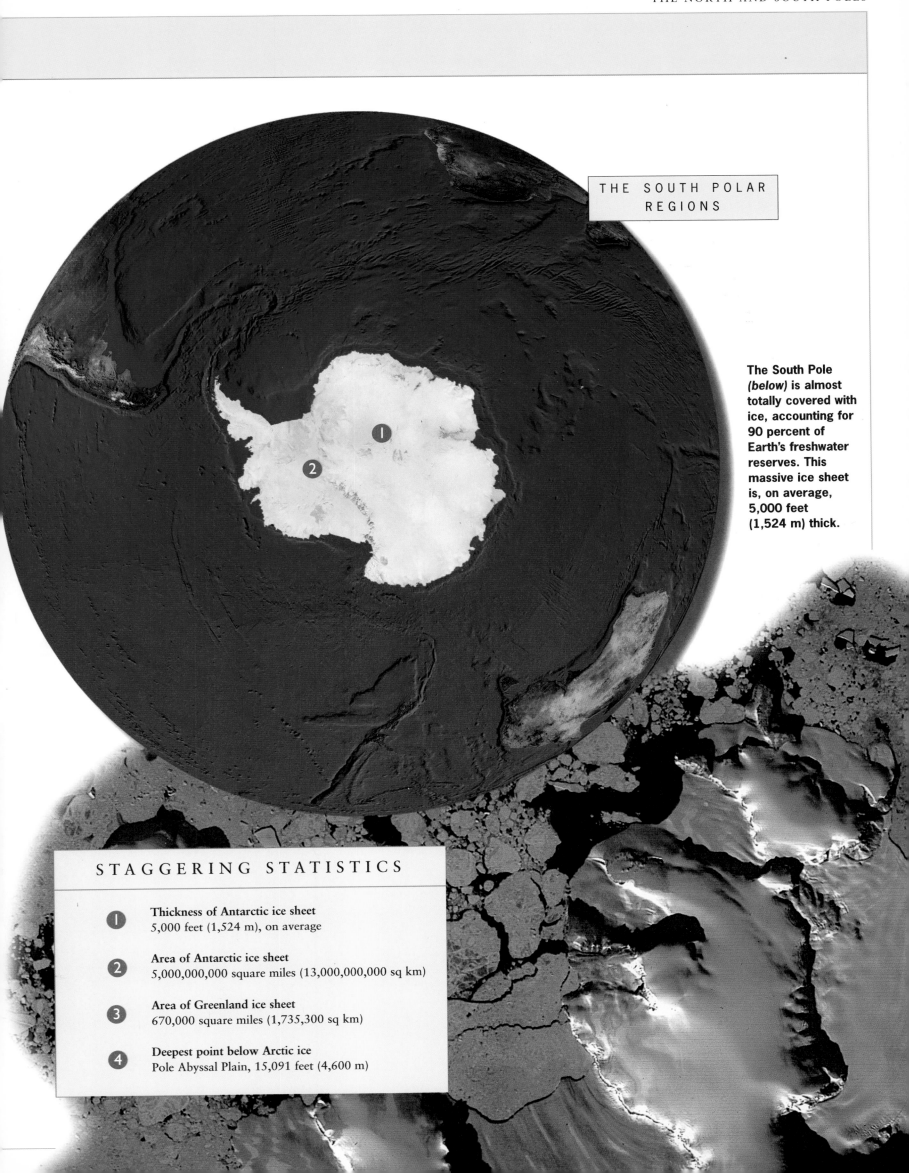

THE SOUTH POLAR
REGIONS

The South Pole
(below) is almost
totally covered with
ice, accounting for
90 percent of
Earth's freshwater
reserves. This
massive ice sheet
is, on average,
5,000 feet
(1,524 m) thick.

STAGGERING STATISTICS

1 Thickness of Antarctic ice sheet
5,000 feet (1,524 m), on average

2 Area of Antarctic ice sheet
5,000,000,000 square miles (13,000,000,000 sq km)

3 Area of Greenland ice sheet
670,000 square miles (1,735,300 sq km)

4 Deepest point below Arctic ice
Pole Abyssal Plain, 15,091 feet (4,600 m)

Glossary

A

Abyssal plain

The flat bed of the ocean between the *continents*, from which *ocean ridges* rise and which dips into *ocean trenches*. The abyssal plain is between 11,500 and 18,200 feet (3,500 and 5,500 m) deep and lies in permanent darkness.

Acid rain

Rain that has become acidic because of chemicals dissolved from the atmosphere. Waste gases given off by factories are a common cause of acid rain. These gases can damage crops and poison *groundwater* downwind from the source of pollution. Acid rain is also caused naturally by the gases that erupt from *volcanoes*.

Alluvium

Loose material, such as sand, mud, or silt, that is deposited by rivers and streams. Some of the most fertile farmland is formed on alluvium deposited by rivers in flood.

Andesitic volcano

A *volcano* that erupts andesitic *lava*, which is relatively rich in the *mineral* silica. This mineral makes the lava thick and easily solidified. Andesitic volcanoes are formed by the action of plate *tectonics*, when one plate overrides another. The *magma* is derived from molten plate material, and eruptions tend to be violent and explosive, in contrast to *basaltic volcanoes*.

Arctic Circle

The theoretical line, at 66° 30 north latitude, within which the Sun does not rise during at least one day of the year, and does not set during at least one day. The equivalent latitude in the Southern Hemisphere is the Antarctic Circle.

Asteroid

Sometimes called a "planetoid," a body of rock, smaller than a planet or a moon, that orbits the Sun in the solar system.

Asthenosphere

A fairly soft layer within Earth's *mantle,* the lubricating layer on which Earth's plates move during the process of plate *tectonics*. The layer that contains the plates of Earth's *crust* is called the *lithosphere*.

Atoll

A ring-shaped *coral* reef formed when an island gradually subsides, allowing any coral reef around the edge to grow, keeping pace with the rate of subsidence. The lagoon that forms in the middle of the reef represents the original area of the island.

B

Basalt

A dark, fine-grained, *igneous rock* that flows out of fissures in *volcanoes* that do not erupt explosively, then cools and hardens. Basaltic *lava* is usually erupted at the bottom of the ocean. It can form lava fields thousands of feet (m) thick.

Basaltic volcano

A *volcano* that erupts basaltic *lava*. Basaltic volcanoes are broad and flat because the lava tends to flow some distance and spread out before solidifying into *basalt* rock. Basaltic volcanoes are found where new plates are being generated. The *magma,* derived from the *mantle,* is low in silica and produces gentle eruptions.

Breaker

An ocean wave that curls over and breaks into surf when it reaches the shallow water along the shore.

British Antarctic Survey

An institute of Britain's Natural Environment Research Council, specializing in the study of Antarctica.

C

Calcite

The *mineral* calcium carbonate ($CaCO_3$), which is the principal ingredient of *limestone*. This mineral is easily broken down by acid in *groundwater*, and its instability accounts for the characteristic *erosion* patterns of limestone landscapes.

Caldera

A very large *crater* caused by the inward collapse of a *volcano* into its *magma* chamber. If the volcano is extinct, this crater will be filled with water.

Canyon

A deep gorge cut by a stream through rock. Canyons are often found in arid areas, such as the southwestern United States, that are subjected to heavy flash floods at certain times of the year.

Cavern

A cave, particularly one formed in a *limestone* terrain.

Chlorofluorocarbon (CFC)

A gaseous compound of chlorine, fluorine, and carbon, used in many industrial processes. CFCs are not easily broken down, and their buildup in the atmosphere can lead to pollution problems because it damages the *ozone layer*.

Cirque

An armchair-shaped hollow formed by glacial erosion in the side of a mountain. A cirque is the place a *glacier* originates. The great weight of its snow and ice grind out the hollow. *Cirque* is a French term

that originally applied to the Alps. In the Scottish Highlands, a cirque is called a corrie; in the Welsh mountains, it is a cwm.

Climate

The metereological conditions of an area, averaged out over a long period of time. Climate differs from weather in that weather is the daily variations in the climate of an area.

Conglomerate

A coarse *sedimentary rock* consisting of rock fragments cemented together.

Coniferous

Describes trees that bear their seeds in cones and usually have leaves in the form of needles. Pine, fir, and spruce are typical examples of coniferous trees.

Continent

A very large landmass.

Continental shelf

The submerged edge of a *continent*, covered by seawater to a depth of about 400 feet (122 m). Beyond this shelf is the continental slope, where the sea becomes deeper very rapidly.

Coral

A tiny, sedentary marine animal, without a backbone, that extracts calcium carbonate from seawater to make a limy external skeleton. Hundreds of thousands of corals, built up on one another, form a reef.

Core

The innermost layer of Earth's structure, made mostly of iron and having two parts – an inner core that is solid and an outer core that is liquid.

Coriolis effect

The process by which anything moving toward the *equator*, such as the wind, is deflected west, and anything moving away

Glossary

from the equator is deflected east. This effect is caused by the rotation of Earth on its axis.

Crater

A circular depression found at the top of a *volcano* or caused by the impact of a *meteorite* that strikes Earth.

Crevasse

A deep crack, especially in the surface of a *glacier*. The rigid surface of a glacier cracks and splits as the glacier flows around a sharp corner of its valley or over a hump on the valley floor.

Crust

The topmost layer of Earth's structure, made of relatively light rocky material, that surrounds the *mantle*. Earth has two types of crust: oceanic crust and continental crust. Oceanic crust is the more dense and forms the floors of the oceans. Continental crust is the only part of Earth's structure we normally see, and it is lighter than oceanic crust. Individual masses of continental crust form the continents and are embedded in oceanic crust. The plates that take part in plate *tectonics* consist of the crust and the topmost layer of the mantle.

Crystal

A piece of a naturally formed *mineral* that has a specific shape, which reflects the arrangement of atoms in the mineral.

D

Deciduous

Describes a tree, such as oak or ash, that loses its leaves in fall and grows new ones in spring.

Delta

An area of *deposition* at the mouth of a river, where sand and silt carried by the river pile up to form a low, swampy plain through which the river cuts channels. A delta forms where there are no sea currents to wash away the deposited material.

Deposition

The process by which material washed along by a river or stream settles on the bottom, when the current slows, and builds up beds of *sediment*.

E

Ecosphere

In an astronomical sense, the theoretical region around the Sun in which it is possible for life as we know it to exist. Also used in the biological sense as meaning Earth and the region within the atmosphere.

Effluent

Industrial waste material, usually in the form of a liquid, such as sewage, or smoke, that is discharged into the environment, often polluting it.

Ejecta

The broken material thrown out by a *volcano* or blasted out by the impact of a *meteorite*.

El Niño

A pattern of weather, that occurs every few years with disastrous effects, caused by a disruption in the normal flow of prevailing winds and currents in the Pacific Ocean.

Epicenter

The point on Earth's surface directly above the focus of an earthquake, where the greatest damage normally occurs.

Equator

The theoretical line around the Earth at 0° latitude.

Erosion

The breaking down and wearing away of rocks and landforms by the actions of the elements, such as wind, waves, river currents, and glacial ice.

F

Fjord

A long, deep, narrow inlet from the ocean, bounded by steep cliffs, which is carved by the action of *glaciers*. Fjords are commonly found on the west coast of Norway.

Fossil

The remains of a plant or animal found preserved in rock, most often in *sedimentary rock*.

G

Glacier

A mass of ice that is built up on land by repeated snowfalls, then moves slowly downhill under the influence of gravity.

Gondwana

The *supercontinent* in the Southern Hemisphere on which South America, Africa, India, Australia, and Antarctica existed until about 50 million years ago. Gondwana gradually split up and the continents slowly moved to their present positions.

Granite

An *igneous rock* consisting of large *crystals* and containing a high proportion of silica in the form of the *mineral* quartz.

Greenhouse effect

The warming of Earth's surface due to the changing composition of the atmosphere, allowing the Sun's rays in and preventing excess heat from radiating out.

Groundwater

Water found under surface *soil*.

Much of the rainwater that falls sinks into the ground, soaking the soil and accumulating at various depths. The depth at which the soil and rocks become saturated with water is known as the zone of saturation. The top level of the water in this zone is called the water table.

Gyre

A vast circular movement of ocean currents.

I

Ice Age

A time when Earth's climate was cooler and ice sheets and *glaciers* were more extensive than they are today. The end of the last Ice Age was about 20,000 years ago.

Ice cap

A *glacier* that is not confined to a valley, but covers a large continental area. Ice caps are found in Antarctica and Greenland, as well as on the Arctic Ocean. Unlike valley glaciers, which move downhill, the movement of an ice cap is outward as new ice from snowfalls accumulates in the center. The terms ice cap and ice sheet are often used interchangeably.

Igneous rock

One of the three main types of rocks that make up Earth's *crust*, this rock forms when hot molten material, such as *magma*, cools and solidifies.

Island arc

An arc-shaped chain of volcanic islands formed on the inside curve of an *ocean trench* through the action of plate *tectonics*.

J

Jet stream

A particularly strong wind,

Glossary

found in the mid latitudes of the stratosphere, blowing eastward at speeds of up to 300 mph (483 kmph). A jet stream is a result of the circulation pattern of the atmosphere around the globe. It is often sought out by long-distance airline pilots to assist their eastward flights.

K

Karst

A very dry form of landscape found in a region of *limestone*, which dissolves easily on exposure, particularly through the action of acidic *groundwater*. Joints or cracks in the rock are dissolved into wide openings, called "grikes," leaving the intervening areas of rock in upstanding blocks called "clints." "Karst" is the name of a limestone region, in the country formerly called Yugoslavia, that is dominated by landforms produced through groundwater solution.

L

Lagoon

A shallow area of seawater partially or totally cut off from the sea by a barrier such as a *coral* reef.

Lava

Molten rocky material that erupts from a *volcano*, then cools and hardens on Earth's surface. Basaltic lava is very fluid and covers long distances before solidifying. Andesitic lava is stiff and easily solidified, so it does not flow very far.

Levee

A raised bank along the side of a river, built up from *sediment* deposited during floods.

Limestone

A type of *sedimentary rock*

consisting mostly of the *mineral* calcium carbonate, or *calcite*.

Lithosphere

The outer shell of Earth that forms the *tectonic* plates. Consisting of the *crust* and the topmost layer of Earth's *mantle*, the lithosphere is solid and moves around on the softer *asthenosphere* below.

Longshore drift

An effect of a sea current, in which sand and pebbles are transported in one direction along a beach. This effect results in *sand bars*, sand spits, and *tombolos*.

M

Magma

Molten rock that exists below Earth's surface, magma is made up largely of silicates and dissolved gases. When magma erupts at the surface through volcanic action, it is called *lava*.

Mantle

This part of Earth's structure lies between the *core* and the *crust* and contains the greatest proportion of Earth's volume. It is solid, made of a stony material, except for a soft layer close to the outside, which provides the lubrication needed for plate *tectonics*.

Marble

A type of *metamorphic rock* formed when *limestone* is subjected to intense heat and pressure.

Meander

A loop formed in a slow-moving river as it crosses a flood plain. As the river winds through *sediments* deposited on the valley floor, the current is always faster on the outsides of the curves, eroding the banks away. On the insides of the curves,

eroded material being carried along is deposited as a beach. In this way, the curve of the river extends itself, in a process known as meandering.

Mediterranean climate

A climate characterized by warm, wet, westerly winds in winter and hot, dry summers. In addition to the Mediterranean countries themselves, South Africa, Southern Australia, parts of Chile, and California also experience this type of climate.

Metamorphic rock

One of the three main types of rocks that make up Earth's *crust*, this rock forms when pre-existing rock is heated or compressed so much that it changes physically or chemically. In the process, however, the rock does not melt. If it did, the result would be *igneous rock*.

Meteorite

A remaining lump of rocky or metallic matter that falls to Earth when a meteor passes through the atmosphere and burns up.

Mineral

One of the constituents of rock; a naturally formed substance that has a particular chemical composition. Pure minerals form *crystals*. A rock might contain a number of different crystals.

N

NASA

National Aeronautics and Space Administration, which is an organization established by the United States in 1958 to administer space exploration.

Neap tide

The tidal condition that occurs twice a month when the gravitational influence of the Sun and the Moon are pulling

at right angles to one another. During neap tides, there is only a small tidal range, with high tides being relatively low, and low tides relatively high.

O

Ocean ridge

A ridge formed along the ocean floor by the upwelling of molten material from beneath the *crust*. New plates are formed on these ridges in the process known as plate *tectonics*.

Ocean trench

An elongated depression in the ocean floor, formed by the process of plate *tectonics*, at the site where an old plate slips down below the one next to it and is destroyed.

Oil trap

An underground rock structure that gathers and concentrates petroleum. Oil geologists spend much of their time looking for oil traps.

Oxbow lake

A curved lake formed by a *meander* in a river that has gradually been cut off by deposits of *sediment*.

Ozone layer

A layer in Earth's atmosphere that is particularly rich in a type of oxygen called ozone. Ozone is important to life on Earth because it helps filter out harmful rays from the Sun. The pollution of industrial gases tends to break down this layer.

P

Peninsula

A long, narrow piece of land extending into a body of water, such as the sea or a large lake,

Glossary

so that it is almost completely surrounded by water.

Permafrost

An underground layer of frozen *soil* that does not thaw, even during the summer. At high latitudes, this layer creates waterlogged landscapes, called *tundra*, where meltwater on the surface cannot drain away through the soil.

Pingo

A landscape feature associated with *permafrost*, consisting of an underground core of ice that expands and pushes upward, forming a soil-covered mound. Pingoes can be up to 200 feet (61 m) high.

R

Reef

A mass of rock or *coral*, or a sandy ridge, that lies just below the surface of the water.

Rift valley

A valley formed as Earth's *crust* stretches, and an area of land subsides between cracks or faults.

Rock cycle

The process whereby rocks are broken down by the forces of weathering and *erosion*, and the debris, which is transported by rivers, *glaciers*, wind, sea currents, and so on, is eventually deposited, buried, and formed into other rocks. In parts of the process, rocks are either heated and compressed deep within Earth to become new rocks, or rocks melt and resolidify into new rocks.

S

Sand bar

A deposit of sand, either underwater or just above the surface, that is formed by the movement of waves and ocean currents.

Savanna

An expanse of dry tropical grassland, with few trees, that borders the equatorial rain forest on both the north and south.

Schist

A type of *metamorphic rock* with a twisted shape and flattened *crystals* that show the pressure under which it was formed.

Scree

Loose rock fragments that have accumulated at the base of a hill or cliff; also called "talus."

Sediment

Loose rocky, sandy, or silty material eroded from the land and deposited on a seafloor, riverbed, or desert basin.

Sedimentary rock

One of the three main types of rocks that make up Earth's *crust*, this rock forms when layers of *sediment* or organic matter are compressed over long periods of time, sometimes along with *minerals* or chemicals, until their particles are cemented together.

Shale

A fine-grained *sedimentary rock* formed by the solidification of mud.

Shield area

A region of ancient *metamorphic rock* found in the heart of a *continent*. These regions are given individual names, such as the Canadian Shield and the Baltic Shield.

Soil

The mixture of broken rocky material and organic debris that forms the surface layer of Earth.

Solstice

The time of the year when the Sun is at its highest point or its lowest point in the sky.

Spring tide

The tidal condition that occurs twice a month when the gravitational influence of the Sun and the Moon are pulling in the same direction. During spring tides, there is a large tidal range, with high tides particularly high and low tides particularly low.

Strata

The series of layers of deposited organic matter that, when compressed over long periods of time, form various kinds of *sedimentary rock*.

Subcontinent

An area of land, such as India, that has the characteristics of a *continent* but is attached to a larger landmass.

Supercontinent

A very large *continent*, usually formed when landmasses come together during the process of plate *tectonics*. A supercontinent may eventually break up into smaller landmasses, again, also by means of plate tectonics.

T

Tectonics

The movement of Earth's surface as a series of plates continually being created as *ocean ridges* and destroyed as *ocean trenches*. These plates are in constant motion, creating geological structures, such as folds and faults; building mountain ranges; and causing earthquakes and volcanic eruptions.

Tombolo

An island connected to a mainland by a *sand bar*.

Trade winds

The prevailing winds that blow toward the equator, generated by warm air rising over the hottest area on Earth, and cooler air to the north and south sweeping in to take its place. These winds do not blow due north and south. They are deflected to the west due to the *Coriolis effect*.

Tundra

In the Northern Hemisphere, the northernmost plains covered with snow and ice that thaws during a brief summer. Because a deep layer of *soil*, called *permafrost*, remains frozen, meltwater on the surface cannot drain away, resulting in a treeless landscape of lakes and marshes.

Typhoon

The local name for a hurricane in the Indian Ocean or the China Sea.

V

Volcano

The vent through which *lava* and *ejecta* erupt during a *tectonic* upheaval. Material builds up around the vent to form a mountain, usually with a *crater* in the top. There are two basic kinds of volcanoes: broad, flat *basaltic volcanoes* and steep-sided, conical *andesitic volcanoes*.

W

Water cycle

The constant movement of water from the oceans through evaporation, into the atmosphere as vapor, onto the land as rain and snow, and back to the oceans by way of rivers.

Additional Resources

More Books to Read

The Breathing Earth
Deep Green Planet (series)
Renato Massa, Monica
Carabella, and Lorenzo
Fornasari
(Raintree/Steck-Vaughn)

Discovering Earthquakes
Nancy Field
(Dog-Eared Publications)

Discovering Volcanoes
Nancy Field
(Dog-Eared Publications)

DK Pockets: Earth Facts
Cally Hall, editor
(DK Publishing)

Earth and Universe
Record Breakers (series)
Storm Dunlop
(Gareth Stevens)

**Earth Dance: How Volcanoes,
Earthquakes, Tidal Waves**

**and Geysers Shake Our
Restless Planet**
Cynthia Pratt Nicolson
(Kids Can Press)

Exploring the World of Geology
Try This! (series)
George Burns
(Franklin Watts)

The Geography of the Earth
Susan Brooks
(Oxford University Press)

Geology: The Active Earth
*Ranger Rick's
Naturescope* (series)
Sandra Stotksy
(Chelsea House)

**Geology Crafts for Kids: 50
Nifty Projects to Explore the
Marvels of Planet Earth**
Alan Anderson, Gwen Diehn,
and Terry Krautwurst
(Sterling Publications)

Glaciers
*First Books: Earth and Sky
Science* (series)
Roy A. Gallant
(Franklin Watts)

Mountains and Volcanoes
World Habitats (series)
Rose Pipes
(Raintree/Steck-Vaughn)

**The New York Public Library
Incredible Earth: A Book of
Answers for Kids**
Ronald Rood, editor
(John Wiley & Sons)

Oceans and Seas
World's Top Ten (series)
Neil Morris
(Raintree/Steck-Vaughn)

**Our Patchwork Planet: The
Story of Plate Tectonics**
Helen Roney Sattler
(Lothrop Lee & Shepard)

Our Planet Earth
*101 Questions and
Answers* (series)
Steve Parker
(Facts on File, Inc.)

Rivers
*Sequences of Earth and
Space* (series)
Andres Llamas Ruiz
(Sterling Publications)

The Satellite Atlas
David Flint
(Gareth Stevens)

**The Sky's the Limit: All Abou:
the Atmosphere**
Mark J. Rauzon
(Millbrook Press)

**The Third Planet: Exploring
the Earth from Space**
Tam O'Shaughnessy
and Sally K. Ride
(Crown Publications)

Videos

Amazing Planet: Lava Blast
(National Geographic Kids)

Born of Fire
(National Geographic)

**Cousteau - Voyage to the
Edge of the World - An**

Arctic Adventure
(United American Video)

Creation of the Universe
(PBS Home Video)

Nova - The Day the Earth Shook
(WGBH Boston Video)

Raging Planet - Hurricane
(Discovery Communication)

Raging Planet - Tornado
(Discovery Communication)

**Rainbow of Stone: A Journey
Through Deep Time in the**

Grand Canyon
(Terra Productions)

**World's Most Dangerous
Volcanoes**
(Simitar Video)

Web Sites

Glacier
www.glacier.rice.edu

National Geographic Xpeditions
*www.nationalgeographic.com/
education/xpeditions/
main.html*

Science 10: Earth Science
*www.educ.uvic.ca/Faculty/
jtinney/earth%20science/
ESmain.html*

VolcanoWorld
volcano.und.nodak.edu

Ocean Planet
*seawifs.gsfc.nasa.gov/
OCEAN_PLANET/HTML/
ocean_planet_ocean_
science.html*

Windows to the Universe
(select **Kids' Space**)
windows.ivv.nasa.gov/

Due to the dynamic nature of the Internet, some web sites stay current longer than others. To find additional web sites, use a reliable search engine with one or more of the following keywords: *astronomy, atmosphere, continents, deserts, Earth, El Niño, erosion, fossils, fuel, geology, glaciers, lakes, minerals, oceans, ozone, planets, pollution, rivers, rocks, solar system, storms, tides, volcanoes, weather.*

Index

Index